Matter a

Matter and Motion

A Brief History of Kinetic Materialism

Thomas Nail

EDINBURGH
University Press

Edinburgh University Press is one of the leading university presses
in the UK. We publish academic books and journals in our selected
subject areas across the humanities and social sciences, combining
cutting-edge scholarship with high editorial and production values to
produce academic works of lasting importance. For more information
visit our website: edinburghuniversitypress.com

Grateful acknowledgement is made to the sources listed in the List of
Figures for permission to reproduce material previously published elsewhere. Every effort has been made to trace the copyright holders, but
if any have been inadvertently overlooked, the publisher will be pleased
to make the necessary arrangements at the first opportunity.

Edinburgh University Press Ltd
The Tun – Holyrood Road
12(2f) Jackson's Entry
Edinburgh EH8 8PJ

Typeset in 11/14pt Bembo
by Cheshire Typesetting Ltd, Cuddington, Cheshire

A CIP record for this book is available from the British Library

ISBN 978 1 3995 2542 8 (hardback)
ISBN 978 1 3995 2543 5 (paperback)
ISBN 978 1 3995 2544 2 (webready PDF)
ISBN 978 1 3995 2545 9 (epub)

Contents

List of Figures

Introduction

This is a book about matter and motion. More specifically, it is a brief genealogy of a single line of ancient and modern thinkers who shared a distinctly different understanding of matter and motion within the Euro-Western tradition. For the most part, thinkers in the Western tradition have thought of matter and motion as relatively inferior phenomena caused by more primary formal or static principles. But why, and what are the origins of this philosophical preference?

My search to answer these questions began about a decade ago when I started studying the history and politics of global migration and mobility. During this time, I became curious about why nearly every Western thinker I read seemed to privilege stasis in one way or another. I wondered why such an abstract philosophical bias seemed to have such enormous consequences for the politics of migration. So I wrote two books trying to work through the political consequences and history of this idea, *The Figure of the Migrant and Theory of the Border*. But the more I dug, the more questions surfaced. Beyond politics, I wondered why almost all Western descriptions of reality, art and science also seem so committed to explaining the movement of matter by something static?

Nearly all the ancient Greek philosophers thought the

1

world was an eternal sphere with a static centre. Newton, Descartes and Leibniz all thought God was like an eternal clockmaker who endowed the world with immutable laws that we could know. Even Einstein believed that we lived in a closed-off 'block universe' with unchanging physical laws.

The more I read and wrote about this pervasive obsession with form and stasis, the more I became curious about the exceptions to the rule within this tradition. Who bucked the trend and why? What did it mean to disagree with the quest for fixed forms of knowledge and what are the consequences of such a disagreement? Suddenly, what I thought was a narrow question about the nature of motion and matter started to look more like a major lynchpin of Western civilisation. There are very few assumptions or commitments that I found to be as culturally pervasive as this, but what are the alternatives?

My search for an answer led me to teach a class called 'The Philosophy of Movement' for several years in a row. The aim of the class was to read various thinkers in the Western tradition who might have thought that matter and motion were ontologically *primary* and not *derived* from some more static and less material principle. Working through the history of philosophy in this way became the basis for my book *Being and Motion*, which, among other things, catalogued all the different ways philosophers had subordinated matter and motion to something more fixed. It also turned out that my hunches about who might be a 'philosopher of motion' in this tradition were all wrong. I thought they would be the so-called 'process philosophers' such as Henri Bergson, Alfred North Whitehead and Gilles Deleuze. But instead, I was surprised to find the Roman poet Lucretius, the German philosopher Karl Marx and the English writer Virginia Woolf walking this aberrant path. The central common thread seemed to be their belief that everything was made of matter in motion and that, explicitly following Lucretius, it swerved indeterminately. Indeed, for these thinkers there was no higher cause, god, form, essence, vital energy or static principle that caused matter to move.

I spent the next eight years investigating and teaching their work more deeply. I wrote three books on Lucretius, and one each on Marx and Woolf. I also discovered a couple of contemporary physicists, Carlo Rovelli and Karen Barad, whose interpretations of quantum mechanics were strikingly consistent with the core ideas of this tradition. But immediately after tracing this lineage, my mind returned to history and two new questions emerged. Where did Lucretius get his idea of the swerve and how did the terms 'matter' and 'motion' enter into Western philosophy in the first place? Surely, Lucretius was not the beginning. So, I spent the next few years tracing the earliest recorded precursors to the Western notions of matter and motion back to Archaic Greece and Bronze Age Crete.

This book is my attempt to tell in brief form the untold history of a relatively rare but philosophically important line of thought in the Western tradition. Not only does this book add two new links to the lineage I have been tracing for the past decade, Minoan and Archaic Greek, it also identifies a key thematic resonance around the three aspects of what I call 'kinetic materialism', that is, 'indeterminacy', 'relationality' and 'process'. Kinetic materialism is the belief that matter and motion are 'indeterminate relational processes'. In the coming chapters, I define each of these terms and show how they were understood by the ancient and modern authors listed above.

This book is an extended essay written for a broad and non-specialist audience with minimal technical jargon and no literature reviews. It is not intended as a complete historical genealogy of materialism or movement in general, nor the ideas of indeterminacy, relationality and process treated separately. Rather, my aim is to trace a lineage of thinkers who have philosophically *integrated* all five ideas of matter, motion, indeterminacy, relationality and process. Any thinker who has not prioritised all five of these ideas *together* does not appear in this book, but is treated elsewhere.[1]

How is the book organised? Instead of proceeding chronologically by thinker, I have organised the chapters thematically around the three ideas of indeterminacy, relationality and process. This is because the aim of this book is to tell an *interpretative history* from the perspective of these very specific ideas as I understand them. The point is not that all these thinkers agreed with one another on everything. The aim is to argue that we might benefit from taking up this tradition in our own way today. And I will say more about the advantages of this shortly.

Each chapter begins with one of these key ideas (indeterminacy, relationality, process) and shows how each idea changes the way the West has typically thought about matter and motion. The rest of each chapter shows how that idea was taken up historically from the Mediterranean and into modern Europe. I would like to show how what I am calling kinetic materialism emerged first in pre-Greek Minoan culture and in Archaic Greek poetry. These directly and indirectly influenced the materialism of the Roman poet Lucretius, writing in the first century BCE. However, Lucretius' only known book, *On the Nature of Things*, then disappeared for over a thousand years.[2] When the Italian humanist Poggio Bracciolini finally discovered it in the fifteenth century, it circulated widely through Europe to great effect.

Interpretations of Lucretius' text varied widely, but in 1841 a young German philosopher named Karl Marx wrote his doctoral thesis on Greek atomism, using Lucretius' poem as his primary text. Marx's interpretation of Lucretius was highly heterodox in that it emphasised all the things that most modern readers did not like in Lucretius, mostly notably his description of matter's indeterminate swerve.

After Marx's admittedly challenging and misunderstood dissertation, Lucretius' poem found another heterodox reader in the English novelist Virginia Woolf. Woolf carefully read and translated parts of Lucretius' influential text as she learned Latin. Shortly before her death, Woolf wrote in her autobiography that the core of her 'philosophy' was the 'moments of being', or poetic ecstasy, that she had found first in Lucretius' poem, along with the idea of the swerve. Today, Lucretius' legacy continues, to some degree, among quantum physicists who explicitly credit him as the philosophical precursor to Einstein's kinetic theory of matter and to quantum indeterminacy.

This is how I have come to understand the genealogy of kinetic materialism in the West so far. In particular, I have come to see Lucretius as extremely important as an intermediary or translator between the ancient and the modern world. Lucretius preserved key ideas from the Archaic world in explicitly philosophical terms that modern readers could hear easily as answers to their own questions. Marx, Woolf and Rovelli all read Lucretius in a way that uniquely tied them together in the longer philosophical sequence that I want to chronicle here. I should also add that I think of my own philosophy of movement as a continuation of this tradition of kinetic materialism.[3] The lineage of the thinkers covered in this book has been a powerful source of inspiration for nearly all my ideas.[4] Indeed, this book draws on my earlier works and puts the genealogy together for the first time.

Why Trace the Genealogy of Kinetic Materialism?

Unfortunately, the Euro-Western tradition has widely defined itself by the progressive domination of nature. It has almost universally assumed the existence of a natural hierarchy in which some things, people and ideas are inferior to others. This is true even when it is not stated explicitly. Modern European scientists and political thinkers justified the treatment of nature, women and colonies with the idea that they were passive material to be manipulated and mastered by the rational minds of white men.[5]

Philosophers placed certain metaphysical categories such as eternity, God, the soul, forms and essences at the 'top' of a hierarchy to explain the movement of matter at the bottom. The top of the hierarchy secured and ordered the bottom. Now, after thousands of years of treating nature and matter as an inactive substance moulded by ideal or rational forms, many people are feeling the ecological consequences of this mistake with global climate change and mass extinction.

For more than a century, 'critical philosophy' has been exposing and challenging these hierarchical assumptions.[6] The premise of this critical theory has been that philosophers can contribute to social and intellectual transformation by showing people the dominating nature of their practical and theoretical assumptions. For example, patriarchy, capitalism, racism and ecocide are not unrelated phenomena. Critical theorists have been arguing for decades that they are interlocking behaviours with shared hierarchical assumptions about reality. Whether or not individuals are consciously aware of it, an imaginary hierarchy passed down from ancient and modern history shapes their thoughts and actions.[7]

This hierarchical logic places stasis above motion, form above matter, life above death, God above humans, humans above nature, men above women, reason above emotion, white skin above brown skin, the first world over the third world, citizens above migrants, straight above queer and humans above animals. At the very bottom of this chain are matter and motion. Everything above rests on their mute receptivity.

My contribution to critical theory in this book is to challenge this hierarchy and the notion that matter and motion are inferior. If all hierarchy rests on the assumption that inferior beings are more material and mutable than those above, showing that matter and motion are not inferior can help undermine this inherited hierarchy. Many humanists and scientists still think of matter as something mechanical, deterministic and passive.[8] However, for decades environmental and feminist philosophers have argued that this hierarchical way of thinking and acting is at least partly to blame for present social inequality and ecological crisis.[9]

Until critical theory turns its tools on the hierarchical chain's last links, even the best critical thinking will remain incomplete and anthropocentric. Without a critical philosophy of matter and motion, theorists may still be able to treat human culture as distinct and superior to nature, and thus justify dominating the planet and humans historically associated with moving matter.

My point in challenging the material base of this hierarchy is not to invert it by showing that matter and motion are superior, but to indicate that the hierarchy is contingent and performative. There is no ontological basis for natural hierarchy, nor for the forms of domination based on it. I admit that the lack of a natural hierarchy does not necessarily stop domination, but it does lift the veil a little so that people can see what is going on. In short, we should move forward knowing that there is no ontologically legitimate justification for social, aesthetic or scientific domination.

Identifying and avoiding hierarchical delusions does not tell us what we *should* do. However, before we can begin to experiment with different ways of living, it will help us immensely to identify and clear out the most dangerous tools in the toolbox. If there is no natural hierarchy, there is no *single* right way to live or guarantee that we will not make mistakes in our experiments. Who 'we are' will change, as will 'what we want'. There is no final metaphysical answer to ethical questions, but only what the Greeks called a *pharmakon*: a practice of steering clear from poisons and experimenting with potential remedies.[10]

There are many ways to survive and flourish with others, and it is no single person's purview to dictate how. The story about matter and motion that I want to tell in this book leaves the good life up to 'us', whoever 'we' may become. Its pharmacological aim is to identify certain poisons to avoid and some possible remedies to try out. A critical history of antiquity to the present can also inspire our imagination of the future and help us experiment with our present.

If we want to survive and flourish on the planet, our best chance is to think and act without metaphysical illusions and dogmatically hierarchal behaviours. Harbouring such fantasies is akin to wearing a blindfold while walking on a tightrope. The blindfold of metaphysical hierarchy can only hinder an already precarious balancing act. Uncovering our eyes does not predetermine our actions or give us an *absolute* view of reality, but it can *help* us get where we want to go without falling. Or, at least, that is how I think of critical theory.

Nature does not compel morality but constrains the material conditions of survival and flourishing in various ways. If we want to survive to try out new forms of life, we need to think and live without delusions about our material situation. But we can't do this if we keep imagining all kinds of metaphysical entities and arbitrary hierarchies that dictate how we play the game. As long as people continue to think and act as though matter and motion are subordinate phenomena, matter and motion can still be wielded as weapons against people and places.[11]

But why return to antiquity to showcase this alternative lineage? If there never were any actual hierarchies or metaphysical entities in nature, how does this genealogy of kinetic materialism help us? History is important here because there is no ahistorical way of knowing. There is no single foundation for knowledge. For instance, quantum physics does not ground or validate Lucretius' idea of the swerve any more than Lucretius' idea validates quantum physics. Each articulates a unique historical dimension of kinetic materialism in its own way.[12]

Furthermore, the history I trace in this book is not intended to be a story of progressive development of knowledge from obscure Minoan rituals to present-day particle colliders. Instead, I want to showcase the points of *conceptual resonance* between different periods, geographies and ways of knowing in religion, poetry, politics, literature and science. Each thinker I discuss in this book offers their own kind of evidence for a world without metaphysics or hierarchy. Each of these thinkers has a theoretical practice that may inspire us today.

Each historical way of knowing presented in this book is one star in the constellation of an alternative philosophy of matter and motion. What we do with this history is up to us, and there are many things we can do with it, and many more buried histories to tell.[13]

Notes

1 This book is not, and cannot be, due to space constraints, an argument for why other thinkers *did not* hold this unique position or why they only held some *part* of it. See Thomas Nail, *Being and Motion* (Oxford: Oxford University Press, 2019). An excellent complementary study to this one for the ancient world is Kojin Karatani, *Isonomia and the Origins of Philosophy*, trans. Joseph A. Murphy (Durham, NC: Duke University Press, 2017). Karatani shows how the idea of self-movement emerged from Hesiod's idea of chaos and was variously augmented and renamed by the early Greek philosophers and ultimately rejected by Plato and Aristotle.

2 For a history of how Lucretius' text was lost, recovered and received, see Stephen Greenblatt, *The Swerve: How the World Became Modern* (New York: W. W. Norton, 2011).

3 Thomas Nail, *The Philosophy of Movement: An Introduction*, under review.

4 I have also been greatly inspired by the work of feminist new materialists, including Stacy Alaimo, Karen Barad and Vicki Kirby. For a full literature review of all the types of new materialism, including its relationship to speculative realism and object-oriented ontology, see Christopher Gamble, Joshua Hanan and Thomas Nail, 'What is New Materialism?', *Angelaki* 24, no. 6 (2019): 111–34.

5 Raj Patel and Jason W. Moore, *A History of the World in Seven Cheap Things: A Guide to Capitalism, Nature, and the Future of the Planet* (Berkeley: University of California Press, 2017).

6 In my view, feminist philosophers have done some of the most important work to trace out this logic. See, for example, Greta C. Gaard and Patrick D. Murphy (eds), *Ecofeminist Literary Criticism: Theory, Interpretation, Pedagogy* (Champaign: University of Illinois Press, 1998); Stacy Alaimo and Susan Hekman (eds), *Material Feminisms* (Bloomington: Indiana University Press, 2008).

7 For an excellent treatment of how the subordination of matter to form is related to political and feminist issues, see Emanuela Bianchi,

The Feminine Symptom: Aleatory Matter in the Aristotelian Cosmos (New York: Fordham University Press, 2014). See also Emanuela Bianchi, Sara Brill and Brooke Holmes (eds), *Antiquities Beyond Humanism* (Oxford: Oxford University Press, 2019).

 8 Gamble, Hanan and Nail, 'What is New Materialism?'.

 9 Serenella Iovino and Serpil Oppermann (eds), *Material Ecocriticism* (Bloomington: Indiana University Press, 2014).

10 See Jacques Derrida, 'Plato's Pharmacy', in *Dissemination*, ed. Barbara Johnson (Chicago: University of Chicago Press, 1981), 61–171.

11 For one recent example of how the historical subordination of matter has justified anti-blackness and white supremacy, see Armond R. Towns, 'Black "Matter" Lives', *Women's Studies in Communication* 41, no. 4 (2018): 349–58. See also Bianchi, *The Feminine Symptom*. For more on the ethical and political consequences of my philosophy of movement, see Thomas Nail, *The Figure of the Migrant* (Redwood City, CA: Stanford University Press, 2015); Thomas Nail, *Theory of the Border* (Oxford: Oxford University Press, 2016); Thomas Nail, *Theory of the Earth* (Redwood City, CA: Stanford University Press, 2021); and Thomas Nail, *Lucretius II: An Ethics of Motion* (Edinburgh: Edinburgh University Press, 2020).

12 For a similar approach, see Gaston Bachelard, *Atomistic Intuitions: An Essay on Classification* (Albany: State University of New York Press, 2018).

13 There are non-Western histories with resonances and experiments on this path as well that I do not trace here. For one of these connections, see Jerry Rosiek, Jimmy Snyder and Scott Pratt, 'The New Materialisms and Indigenous Theories of Non-Human Agency: Making the Case for Respectful Anti-Colonial Engagement', *Qualitative Inquiry* 26, no. 3–4 (2019): 331–46.

I. Indeterminacy

Chapter 1

Ancient Indeterminacy:
Minoan Metamorphosis, Hesiod's Khaos
and Lucretius' Swerve

What are matter and motion? We cannot understand one without the other because everything that moves is material, and all matter is in motion.[1] The most frequent image that comes to mind for most of us when we first think of matter and motion, however, is of something moving along a line from point A to point B.

We think of point A and point B as discrete locations in space, and we think of movement as the successive change in location from one point to another. Let's call this definition of matter and motion 'extensive', because it occurs in extended space with a length, width and depth. It assumes that space and time pre-exist the matter that moves through them. It also typically assumes that the matter that moves is already in some determinate form and was caused by some force. This extensive definition of matter and motion is the dominant one in the Western tradition, even among materialists.

However, this is not the only way to think about matter and motion. In this chapter and the next we take a look at

Figure 1.1 Movement is commonly understood as a translation in discrete spacetime between two static points A and B.

15

the history of an alternative and much less well understood view. We walk through the strange and fascinating history of the idea that matter and motion are 'indeterminate' and what this means for certain understandings of religion, poetry, politics, literature and science.

But first, let's try to define the idea of indeterminacy more clearly and see precisely how it changes our understanding of matter and motion.

What is Indeterminacy?

In the Western tradition, we are used to defining *determinate* beings. According to the Oxford English Dictionary, a 'determinate' being is one with distinct and definite limits. We typically define a 'being' as something that exists as a positive presence.[2] But what if we are trying to talk about something without definite limits and without a fully positive presence? We could use the words 'absence' or 'non-being'. But there is also a third option. We can talk about a 'process' to indicate an event that is neither a determinate being nor a non-being. For example, a swallow swooping after a bug through the sky is neither fully present nor fully absent. It is an 'indeterminate process'.

Indeterminacy, in my view, is a process understood *as a process*, not as a change *of something else* – that is, not as a sequence of changes between static beings. Indeterminacy is not indeterminate *relative* to something determinate. In this view, everything is a process, not just swallows swooping for bugs. Nor should we assume that humans and their thoughts about things are any less indeterminate than everything else. Indeterminacy is an idea but it is more primarily a theoretical performance that we do in the world. As such, we and our ideas and books about indeterminacy also perform it at the same time as they describe it. In this sense, indeterminacy, as I am defining it, is not relative to a circumscribed human-centric view, since indeterminacy does not assume the existence of a circumscribable or fully determinate human. If humans are the world and cannot be separated from it, anthropocentrism is not ontologically possible. However, the danger is that people think and act as though it is. The world is made of processes whose relatively stable iterations and fluctuations generate the metastable phenomena we see around us, including ourselves.

In the Western tradition, most philosophers have placed matter and motion at the bottom of their conceptual hierarchies because they believed matter was so easily and completely shaped by any form that touched it. What matter was 'in itself' was unknown, unlimited and indeterminate. In the Western story, motion is at the bottom of the hierarchy because it is the name for the *process* by which one determinate thing changed into another. The process of motion was not 'nothing' but it wasn't fully 'something' either. So thinkers in this tradition treated motion instead as a series of discrete changes between discrete beings on an unchanging background. Change was ontologically secondary or accidental to the determinate being that changed. This understanding made motion much easier to define but also to locate as an effect of a more primary determinate cause.[3]

But what if matter and motion remained *indeterminate* instead? It would not be a translation from point A to point B, because there would be no determinate point called 'A' nor a fixed object moving through a fixed space and time. 'Point A' would be a continually changing process, and indeterminate matter would have no internal static identity. Matter would not be stuff, substance or a

17

determinate object, but rather a regional stability-in-motion or pattern-in-process. Matter would change what it was when it moved.

From an indeterministic perspective, movement is not a change in empty space from point A to point B. Movement is the continual transformation of the whole extended space, point A, point B and the line. Everything moves and changes indeterminately but in relatively stable iterative patterns. We will return to this idea of patterns in Chapter 5.

Now let's look at how some of the earliest expressions of kinetic materialism articulated the nature of this indeterminacy.

Ancient Indeterminacy

The history of materialism is difficult to trace back prior to the invention of the word 'matter'. The English word 'matter' came from the Latin word *materia*, which meant 'trees' or 'wood', derived from the Latin word *mater* or 'mother'. And the Latin use of *materia* to mean 'matter in general' came from the Classical Greek philosopher Aristotle, who was the first to use the Greek word *húlē*, literally meaning 'forest or wood', to mean instead 'matter in general'.

What did Aristotle mean by *húlē*? He wrote that, 'by matter [*húlē*] I mean that which in itself is neither a particular thing nor a quantity nor sayable or knowable by any of the categories of determinate Being ... Nor indeed is it the negations of these; for the negations too will only apply to it accidentally.'[4]

Specifically, Aristotle wrote that matter was 'unspeakable and irrational' (*mēdén legetai*) and not 'determinate' (*horízō*). He also argued that philosophers who deny the determinacy of being and the principle of non-contradiction are 'stating something indeterminate' (*to aoriston*).[5] This is why Aristotle disagreed with the philosophers of indeterminacy and instead defined matter as a purely passive receiver of superior forms. For Aristotle, form gives indeterminate matter order and purpose.[6]

But why did Aristotle choose the word *hūlē* to mean 'unspeakable indeterminate matter in general'? He could have used many other words for the same purpose. One reason may have been that his teacher Plato did something similar.[7] In the *Timaeus*, Plato used the Greek word *chora*, literally meaning 'countryside',[8] to describe a process with erratic movements, no determinate being, but which passively received the forms given to it by a divine craftsman.[9] Plato may have chosen the word *chora* for this cosmological role because of how the Classical Greeks understood the countryside. For them, the countryside was an empty area or space outside the city that they divided up into private parcels for their use. The *chora* was passive material or empty space ready to receive the form of Greek civilisation.

However, the *chora* meant something quite different for the Archaic Greeks of Homer's time. According to the historian David Asheri, the peripheral zones of the countryside 'were used commonly (as undivided, *koinē chōra*)'.[10] Instead of dividing up the meadows, forests and mountains into private parcels, the Archaic Greeks used them as collective commons for foraging, pasturage and religion.[11] Only much later did the Classical Greeks transform the *chora* into a divided 'administrative province'.[12]

According to the French linguist Emmanuel Laroche, 'the pasture in archaic times is generally an unlimited space; this can be a forest, meadow, river, or mountain side'.[13] Laroche carefully shows how Homer and other Archaic authors used the Greek root *nem* to describe the countryside or *chora* as something 'distributed/shared' among everyone without division or limit. He argued that 'The idea [that the Greek word *nomos* meant] law is a product of fifth- and sixth-century Greek thought.' So Classical Greeks such as Plato shifted the meaning of the word *nomos* from the original Homeric root νεμω meaning, 'I distribute' or 'I arrange',[14] just as they changed the meaning of *chora* from something undivided and common to something divided up, formed and administered. For Laroche, even 'the [retroactively] proposed translations "cut-up earth, plot of land, piece" are not suitable in all cases to the Homeric poems and assume an ancient νεμω "I divide" that we should reject'.[15]

Further, the legal historian Thanos Zartaloudis has written a careful and well-researched book on the idea that the Archaic Greeks understood the countryside as 'undivided' and 'distributed-shared'.[16] The architectural theorist Maria Theodorou has also carefully looked at all usages of the word *chora* in Homer, and concluded that 'Choros in Homer is not related to separation, or to the distinction between, for instance, inside and outside, or open and closed.'[17]

Therefore, Plato chose to use the word *chora* in part because it also meant 'space' and is related to the verb *khoreo*, 'give way' or 'make space', which is a key theme in the *Timaeus*. But the Classical meaning of the word *chora* for Plato as empty passive space was related to the historical division and development of a previously undivided Archaic countryside. Indeed, this is also why Aristotle interpreted Hesiod's use of the word *khaos*, which will discuss below, to mean *chora*. Plato and Aristotle's understanding of 'matter' was therefore shaped by their geographical relationship to their historical countryside and a corresponding change in the use of the Greek word.

What is most important for our story here is the significant connection between the philosophical concept of 'matter', as we understand it today, and its original conceptual origins in the mountains, forests, pastures and rivers of the Archaic countryside. Plato and Aristotle understood that *hûlē* and *chora* originally had more indeterminate meanings, but just as the Greek word shifted, so did their understanding of matter into something that could be cut, formed or made determinate.

But can we trace the Archaic idea of indeterminacy even further back before Homer and Hesiod to the Bronze Age island of Crete? What was the Minoan relationship to the countryside with its undivided forests and mountains, and what might this tell us about their understanding of indeterminacy, transformed into 'matter' by Classical philosophers?

Minoan Metamorphosis

The Greek idea of indeterminacy may have had some of its oldest historical roots in the idea of Minoan *ambiguity*. The Minoans were a diverse group of peoples who lived on Crete from the Neolithic period 130,000 years ago to 1100 BCE. Here I discuss only the early and middle periods between 2700 and 1500 BCE.

The Minoans had a written language, but unfortunately no one has yet deciphered their writing system, known as 'Linear A'. We only have the deciphered fragments of the later related system, 'Linear B', left by a group of people called the Mycenaeans. The Mycenaeans were the first distinctively Greek people, who lived on Crete and in mainland Greece from about 1450 BCE onwards. Further, the Mycenaean language is significant because it contains the earliest known form of the Greek language,[18] including the first recorded names of several Greek gods.

Around 1150 BCE, the Mycenaean civilisation on Crete collapsed for reasons that are still debated among scholars, but which may have involved invasion by other peoples.[19] Scholars call the transition period between the fall of Mycenae and the rise of eighth-century Archaic Greek culture the 'Greek Dark Ages' because of its reduced population and cultural production.

Through the Mycenaeans, Minoan religious practices had a significant influence on Greek culture.[20] Minoan religion was unique compared to other Mediterranean religions because the Minoans did not build monumental temples or depict the worship of any particular god or hero.[21] There was some cult activity in their palaces, but they widely gathered in underground caves, wooded forests and on mountain peaks to perform ecstatic rituals. Minoan religious artefacts depict anonymous human figures in open natural areas shaking trees, sitting under trees, hugging boulders, holding psychoactive poppy pods, raising their arms and dancing in ritual ecstasy around wild plants. Artefacts also depict various animals, plants, insects, humanoid figures and partial objects floating and mixing in the air around the worshippers.[22]

Evidence strongly suggests that the Minoans had no consistent set of attributes for identifying gods, as we see in Egypt, the Near East and Classical Greece.[23] Whatever the sacred was for the Minoans, current evidence indicates that it did not take the form of a god or person.[24] Indeed, the artists who engraved these sacred ritual images intentionally obscured the faces of the people participating in the rituals. Often they removed the heads of human figures entirely, leaving only a tiny prong that rendered them highly ambiguous.[25] On the other hand, the artists recorded bodily movements, subtle gestures, plants and clothing in stunning detail.

According to the Minoan archaeologist Robert Koehl, the 'most profound symbol of Minoan religion, the double axe' was also a deeply 'ambiguous' image. It had the form of a 'visual palindrome', Koehl says, with the same pattern back and forth as well as up and down (see figure 1.2).[26] Minoan pottery, too, used a similarly ambiguous motif of

Figure 1.2 Spiral, rosette and double-axe motifs on *pithoi*. From upper left to middle left: three Knossian 'palace style' *pithoi* (Late Minoan II). Middle right: *pithos* from Knossos (Late Minoan IA). Lower left: *pithos* from Pseira (Late Minoan IA). Lower right: 'palace style' *pithos* (Late Minoan II) from Knossos.

interlocking double spirals wrapped around vessels to create images without determinate beginning or end.[27]

One of the most ambiguous features of Minoan religion was the depiction of the hybridisation and metamorphosis of plants and animals. Such renderings 'pervaded Minoan imagery, go[ing] well beyond the conventional repertoire of fantastic creatures that abound in Egyptian and Near Eastern culture, if only by their variety and singularity'.[28] This was 'exemplified most strikingly by the oeuvre of the "Zakros Master"'.[29] Zakros was a Minoan city on Crete where certain carvings depicted hybrid figures combining female human bodies with parts of birds, goats, lions, and trees in cult images (figs 1.3–1.6).[30] One incredible image seems to show a liminal stage or transformation process

Figure 1.3 Clay sealing from Zakros, Crete. CMS II.7 No. 126. Corpus der minoischen und mykenischen Siegel.

Figure 1.4 Clay sealing from Zakros, Crete. CMS II.7 No. 145 b. Corpus der minoischen und mykenischen Siegel.

between determinate states of human and non-human forms (fig. 1.7).[31] In another image of metamorphosis, one Minoan artist depicted a woman as a butterfly, a typical transformation figure (fig. 1.8).[32] The most famous Minoan metamorphic hybrid, though, was the half-human, half-bull Minotaur (figs 1.9–1.12).[33] Minoan artists frequently depicted the Minotaur in 'contorted poses of exaggerated movement',[34] emphasising the process of transformation.[35]

In short, these artefacts, along with many others, strongly suggest to Koehl and other archaeologists that 'in the realm of religious imagery ambiguity seems to have been a governing principle'.[36] Koehl defines Minoan ambiguity as a fundamental 'uncertainty … in or between two

Figure 1.5 Clay sealing from Zakros, Crete. CMS II.7 No. 177. Corpus der minoischen und mykenischen Siegel.

states of existence'.[37] And based on the archaeological evidence, Koehl argues that ambiguity and metamorphosis were 'profoundly ingrained', 'pervasive' and 'quintessentially Minoan traits'.[38] While perhaps not strictly identical with later Greek definitions of indeterminacy, Minoan ambiguity was likely a significant precursor to it as well as a possible influence.

But what philosophical conclusions can we draw from the apparent proclivity towards ambiguity and metamorphosis in Minoan religion? The Minoans seem to have been interested in an uncertainty in the nature of things as they transformed into one another. That they conducted their religious rituals in non-urban spaces even after they had built palaces suggests that they continued to view certain

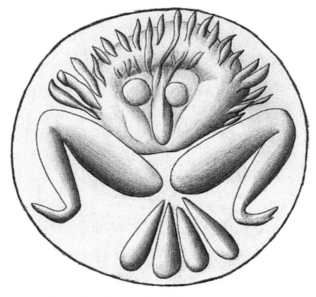

Figure 1.6 Clay sealing from Zakros, Crete. CMS II.7 No. 119. Corpus der minoischen und mykenischen Siegel.

non-urban areas as sacred sites of ambiguous change or metamorphosis. Their creation of ambiguously oriented religious objects such as the double axe, the interlocking double spiral and hybrid creatures also suggests that processes of 'uncertainty ... in or between two states of existence' were significant to their view of the world.

By contrast, it is common in Western thought to give 'ontological priority to *things* over *relations* between them and to *form* over *process*', as the archaeologist Vesa-Pekka Herva argues.[39] But, according to Herva, Minoan religion challenges us to think about ritual more as a material and ecological process without proper temples or divinities. What if the trees, rocks, hybrid creatures and nature-sanctuaries that the Minoans depicted on their artefacts were not symbols or

Figure 1.7 Clay sealing from Zakros, Crete. CMS II.7 No. 170. Corpus der minoischen und mykenischen Siegel.

representations of mental forms of worship or metaphysical entities, but collective agents of a hybrid landscape—human *process*?[40] Minoan ritual seems much less functional or contemplative than crop planting or deity worship respectively, and more like a way for an ecosystem to know/become itself as a hybrid natural—cultural process.

In trying to understand Minoan religion we might take inspiration from the Israeli anthropologist Nurit Bird-David, who has helped shift anthropological thinking away from the idea of animism as about the *independent* agency of non-human persons, and towards a 'new animism' of relational agencies and ambiguous ecologies.[41] For Bird-David, animate agents are not autonomous or discrete but are better understood as aspects or dimensions of broader *processes*.

Figure 1.8 Butterfly seal impression from Zakros, Crete.

In connection with the related 'ontological turn' in anthropology, I am inclined, with others,[42] to interpret Minoan ritual and the images above as engaging with *ambiguous relational processes* and *not* supernatural or transcendent deities.

By placing Minoan ritual in the history of what we call 'matter' and 'motion', I am trying to show how their ambiguous and process-based understandings of reality preceded Plato and Aristotle's passive and discrete definitions of matter and motion. All the archaeological evidence from Minoan Crete during the early and middle periods strongly suggests that the Minoans did not think that the nature of things was made by the imposition of static forms upon passive material. Rather, in Minoan art and religious artefacts, nature seems to trans*form* without beginning or end like the double axe and double spiral.

Figure 1.9 Gold ring, Knossos, Crete. AM 2237, CMS VI.2, No. 336. Corpus der minoischen und mykenischen Siegel.

Figure 1.10 Seal from Phaistos, Crete. CMS III, No. 336. Corpus der minoischen und mykenischen Siegel.

Figure 1.11 Stone seal from Chania, Crete. CMS VS3, No. 150. Corpus der minoischen und mykenischen Siegel.

But how might a similar idea of indeterminacy continue for the Archaic Greeks?

Hesiod's Khaos

In the eighth century BCE, the Greeks still practised religion in both urban and numerous non-urban spaces. Many cult sites of this period were located just on the boundary between urban areas and uninhabited ones, but this does not necessarily mean that there was any absolute boundary between urban and non-urban.[43] Non-urban cult sites often involved built structures, and the historian Vincent Scully has argued that 'all important Greek sanctuaries grew up around open altars which were normally sited where they are because the place itself first suggested the

31

Figure 1.12 Stone seal from Chania, Crete. CMS VS3, No. 154. Corpus der minoischen und mykenischen Siegel.

presence of a divine being. Indeed, its natural forms were regarded as embodying that presence.'[44] Archaeological evidence shows that these Archaic places were sacred locations of epiphany, prophecy, ambiguity and metamorphosis, just as they probably were for the Minoans. One major difference, though, is that the Greeks began singing about *particular* gods and goddesses during this time and built a few temples.

However, it is not by accident that the oldest Greek oracle was a tree cult, and the mother and father of the gods were *tree gods*. The name of this earliest Greek oracle was Dodona and it was founded by the Mycenaeans around 1200 BCE.[45] Dodona was a sacred oak tree located in a region called Epirus in north-western Greece. It was dedicated to Zeus and the mother goddess Dione, and attended by several priestesses in an undeveloped clearing.[46] Written records show that Dodona was a tree cult where priestesses would gather around an oak and listen to its leaves, or perhaps to wind chimes that may have hung from its branches. The tree then whispered its oracular secrets and the priestesses would translate them for others. In particular, the archaeologist Caroline Tully has drawn important similarities between Minoan tree cults and the tree cult at Dodona.[47]

And still by the eighth century BCE, Dodona had no built temple. Priests and priestesses slept on the ground in the sacred grove to better hear the voice of the god. It was only much later in the fourth century BCE that the priests built a small stone temple.[48] As the famous Greek religion scholar Walter Burkert wrote, 'The tree is more important than the stone in marking the sanctuary.'[49] Vincent Scully echoes this idea when he says, 'The place itself is holy and, before the temple was built upon it, embodied the whole of the deity as a recognized natural force.'[50]

Hesiod, a major Greek poet of the Archaic period, wrote about how the Greeks came to worship Zeus at Dodona because of an old connection with Crete. In Hesiod's myth, Gaia, the Earth goddess, gave Metis, the shape-changing river goddess, to Rhea, the 'flowing' (*rheo*) mother goddess, to help Rhea figure out how to save her expected baby Zeus from being eaten by her husband, Cronos. According to Hesiod, Metis was known as 'she who knows most of gods and mortal men',[51] and she gave Rhea the idea of wrapping a rock in a blanket, instead of Zeus, to feed to Cronos. The Greek word *metis* means 'intelligence', 'cunning', 'skill/craft', and the Greek term *mē tis* can also be a pun on the word *outis*, meaning 'no one' or 'nothing'.[52] It is a fitting name for a shape-changer and reveals the important relationship between knowledge and metamorphosis in Archaic Greek culture.[53]

In Hesiod's myth, Metis 'shape-changes' the baby into a rock and outsmarts Cronos, while Rhea flees to the oldest city in Crete, Lyctus, to have her baby. There, Gaia takes the baby Zeus and hides him deep underground on the most sacred wooded hillside of Minoan cult activity: Mount Ida. The Greek word *ide*, which appears already in Homer, means 'tree, wood, or wooded hillside'.[54] Moreover, Gregory Nagy has argued that the name Ida and the phrase Ida Mater can be read already in two Linear A texts *i-da* and *i-da-ma-te*, meaning 'mother goddess of Ida', whose tree-cult rituals took place on the forested mountain bearing her name.[55]

Hesiod gives a beautiful description of the whole event in his *Theogony*.

> [Gaia and Ouranos] sent [Rhea] to Lyctus, to the rich
>   land of Crete,
> when she was about to bear her youngest son,
> great Zeus; vast Earth received him from her
> in wide Crete to tend and raise.
> Carrying him through the swift black night, she came
> first to Lyctus; taking him in her arms, she hid him
> in a deep cave, down in dark holes of holy earth,
> on Mount Aegean [Ida], dense with woods.[56]

In this way, Hesiod posits a mythical connection between Zeus's birth from a Minoan tree cult on Crete and his arrival at Dodona. Of course, the geographical and historical movements of real people and ideas from Crete to Dodona probably did not proceed in such a direct way.

Yet it remains significant that Dodona's location on the wooded hillsides of Epirus also bears a striking resemblance to the forested cave on Mount Ida. The Greeks originally worshipped Zeus at Dodona as a mountainous tree god of oracular vision, and Hesiod at least seems to have noticed its similarity with the history of goddess–tree worship on Crete. For Hesiod, then, the birth of this tree god (Zeus) came directly from the older Minoan and Mycenaean figures of chthonic and metamorphic intelligence, which the Greeks eventually made into the goddesses Rhea, Gaia and Metis.

What do early Greek tree cults have to do with matter and indeterminacy? In his *Theogony*, Hesiod gave a unique name to the first primordial god, '*khaos*'. 'First of all, Chaos came into being [*génet*]', says Hesiod.[57] *Khaos* is an Archaic Greek word whose linguistic root and definition are ultimately unknown, although most scholars agree that its origins are pre-Greek. Hesiod was the first to use this word, but says very little about it. This is why even Greeks writing about *khaos* after Hesiod disagreed widely about what Hesiod might have meant.[58] Modern interpreters, though, have largely tended to define it based on its similarity to two other Greek words, *khaínō* and *kháskō*, which mean 'to yawn, gape, open'. According to the *American Heritage Dictionary of Proto-Indo-European Roots*, these words, and likely the word *khaos*, all came originally from the Proto-Indo-European root *ghēu*, meaning 'to yawn, gape'.[59] Accordingly, many Greek scholars[60] have chosen to think of *khaos* as a 'chasm' that divided a *pre-existing space* or unity between sky and earth. Other recent readers of Hesiod have similarly aimed to make sense of him through the monistic idea that order *inevitably* emerged out of a unified chaos.[61]

The problem, however, according to the classicist Robert Mondi, is that the unquestioned etymology of *khaos* from *khaínō* and *kháskō* has been a red herring, leading to a predetermined interpretation.[62] Etymology dictionaries do not agree on the root word for *khaos* and list two *separate* cross-referenced entries.[63] Frisk's Greek etymology dictionary explicitly says that 'it can only be a distant relationship'.[64] More importantly, Mondi writes,

> even if all these words can be derived ultimately from a single Indo-European root, this fact alone would by no means compel us to think that for Hesiod *khaos* meant the same thing as *khasma* – that is, that he imagined it concretely as a gap or chasm – unless there is some contextual reason to think so.[65]

Just because the root of the word *khaos* might mean 'gap' does not mean that the word *khaos* itself also means 'gap'. This is true of all etymology. Roots do not dictate the precise meaning of their different descendants. Furthermore, Hesiod himself may have made novel use of the term for his own unique cosmogonic purposes.

In short, Hesiod's text itself alone offers the best way to understand what he meant by *khaos*. I have treated this question at length elsewhere and find, largely in agreement with Mondi, that Hesiod intended for *khaos* to be indeterminate, dark, formless and creative.[66] In other words, *khaos* strongly resembles the dark *cave* on Mount Ida's wooded hillside that opened up to the unlimited space beneath the 'roots of the earth' where Zeus was born.[67] Beneath Mount Ida, all is dark, indeterminate, formless and creative. Accordingly, some scholars have argued that the 'Hesiodic word *khaos* is a lexical ancestor of the later physical and philosophical term *húlē* because it conveys the primeval notion of "matter"'[68] as an 'indeterminate chaos'[69] or 'indeterminate element that develops (spatially rather than temporally) into a tangle of determinate elements'.[70]

Other ancient Greek poets, including Homer, similarly described woods and forests with the phrase *aspeton hûlē*, meaning forests that are 'unspeakable, inexpressible concerning size, numbers, or quality; hence, immense, endless'.[71] In this way, Archaic poets of Homer's time explicitly associated *hûlē* with indeterminacy. In the 'Hymn to Dionysus', for instance, the anonymous poet says that Dionysus, also called *Dendritēs* or 'he of the trees', roams loudly through the indeterminate forests (*aspeton hûlē*) after being born from a cave on Mount Ida.

After reading Homer and Hesiod, it makes sense that Aristotle would then write in his *Physics* that *hûlē*, *khaos* and *kenon* (void) were 'indeterminate'.[72] Many scholars have also noted the striking similarities between Hesiod's concept of *khaos* and Plato's use of the word *chora* to refer to an indeterminate generative void associated with the open space and erratic movements of the countryside.[73]

In this way, we can speculate that Minoan religious understandings of forests, caves and mountains as places of ambiguity and metamorphosis may have influenced Archaic Greek conceptions of matter as explicitly 'indeterminate' wilderness (*aspeton hûlē*, *khaos* and *chora*). This, in turn, may have shaped the way Plato and Aristotle understood the older poetic tradition of indeterminacy that they wanted to reject. Perhaps the sacred woods of Archaic Greece were truly 'a place where the logic of distinction goes astray', as one scholar of ancient forests remarks.[74] It was this Archaic indeterminacy that the Classical Greeks wanted to urbanise, formalise and philosophically overthrow.

Lucretius and the Swerve

The first-century BCE Roman poet Lucretius read Homer, Hesiod and the Homeric poets alongside the Greek materialist philosophers Empedocles and Epicurus. Lucretius adopted many ideas from Epicurus, but also left others behind.[75] He took up the poetic idea of material indeterminacy from the Archaic tradition and mixed it with the materialism of the early Greek philosophers in his own way. One result was his description of the 'swerve'.[76]

In his beautiful philosophical verse epic called *De Rerum Natura* (*The Nature of Things*), Lucretius explicitly brought together the ideas of matter and indeterminacy. However, instead of saying that they were caused or formed by some higher and more static principle, he said that they formed themselves by swerving. Readers have often translated and interpreted Lucretius' poem as if he were saying that matter was made of discrete indivisible particles called 'atoms'. Yet it's important to note that Lucretius did not use the Greek word *átomos* or the Latin cognate *atomus*. He did not even use the Latin word *particula*, meaning 'particle', to describe matter.[77] I am not the first scholar to notice this as a meaningful difference between Lucretius and others in the atomist tradition.[78] Elsewhere I have tried to show all the evidence for and consequences of this key difference.[79]

Instead of atoms or particles, Lucretius chose three words much more deeply connected with the Archaic understanding of indeterminate matter: *materia*, *corpora* and *semina*. The Latin word *materia*, as I said above, meant 'wood' and came from the Latin word for 'mother'. This makes perfect sense as a possible influence from Minoan and Archaic Greek cultures where women worshipped trees at Ida and Dodona. *Corpora* is the plural of *corpus*, meaning 'the bodily trunk or shaft of something' or 'the wood under the bark of a tree'. Finally, the Latin word *semina* can mean a 'grafted tree branch', 'shoot', 'seed' or 'sprout', according to the Oxford Latin Dictionary.

Lucretius described a world where branching flows of matter were *infinitum*, meaning 'boundless', literally 'not determinate' in space or time.[80] Similar to Hesiod's description of chaos, Lucretius also sang that the universe emerged from a 'huge shapeless heap of turbulent creativity' (*tempestas quaedam molesque coorta*) and over time became increasingly stable.[81] For Lucretius, as matter flows and branches, it interweaves and alternates to create *inane* or relatively 'empty spaces', which one might compare with how the Greek words *khaos* or *chora* were widely understood as 'indeterminate spaces'.

However, Lucretius' most significant contribution to the idea of material indeterminacy was 'the swerve'. Many readers ancient, modern and contemporary have attributed the swerve originally to Epicurus. But it is important to remember that today we have no extant text from Epicurus where he mentions it. Epicurus wrote letters to Herodotus, in which he aimed to lay out his core philosophical system for students to memorise, but nowhere did he mention the swerve. Not even the careful ancient biographer of philosophers, Diogenes Laertius, wrote anything about a swerve in Epicurus' philosophy. Epicurus' philosophy apparently works just fine without the swerve, according to his own letters. However, other Greek-speaking ancient philosophers such as Philodemus, Diogenes of Oenoanda, Plutarch and Simplicius all say that Epicurus mentioned a swerve.[82]

Why, then, did Epicurus not mention or make use of the swerve in his extant writings on freedom?[83] It is possible that we may discover a mention of a swerve in Epicurus' lost

book *On Nature.* Yet based on the known titles of its chapters
and their extant fragments it seems more likely to me that the
swerve was more fundamental, systematic and developed in
Lucretius' philosophy than it was in Epicurus'. This is what I
have tried to show elsewhere in my books on Lucretius.

Lucretius said that matter is 'accustomed to swerving'
without any external cause 'only a tiny bit, lest we seem
to be inventing oblique movements'.[84] This is a point that
Lucretius' interpreters and critics seem never to have been
able to swallow, that *matter moves without any external cause.*[85]
For Lucretius, the movement of matter is *self-caused.*

Lucretius also says that the swerve occurs

> at times completely indeterminate
> and in indeterminate places they swerve a little from their
>   course,
> but only so much as you could call a change of motion[86]

Matter changes, modulates or deviates[87] its motion[88] to the
smallest possible degree[89] at an indeterminate space and time
before any measurable discrete time or space (*incerto tempore ferme incertisque locis spatio*).[90] According to the Oxford
Latin Dictionary, the word *incerto* means 'undetermined,
not fixed, dubious, unsettled, or indefinite'. For Lucretius,
matter is constantly swerving and branching like a tree, and
the movement is always indeterminately swerving. This is
an idea with clear resonances in the Archaic Greek notions
of *aspeton hū́lē, khaos* and *chora.* Lucretius read and refer-
enced Homer and Hesiod extensively in his poem and was
almost certainly influenced by their understanding of indeterminacy in his description of swerving matter. I have tried
to show elsewhere in greater detail how Lucretius mixed
many poetic ideas with Epicurus' materialism, to create a
more indeterminate materialism.

So, although it may not ever be possible to reconstruct fully the precise historical line of *direct* influence and descent from the Minoans to Lucretius, my aim in this chapter has been to show at least one plausible series of connections among different Greek names for indeterminacy. My tentative conclusion is that what we now call 'matter' and 'motion' at one point meant 'indeterminacy' for the Greeks.

In the next chapter, the genealogical road becomes a bit clearer as we have vastly more written documents recording the lines of influence. Lucretius' debt to Archaic poetry is explicit, but the influence of Lucretius on modern philosophers is even more explicit. So in the next chapter, we see how the idea of indeterminate materialism passed from Lucretius to the modern thinkers of kinetic materialism.

Notes

1 See Thomas Nail, *Theory of the Object* (Edinburgh: Edinburgh University Press, 2021).

2 Jacques Derrida, *Of Grammatology* (Baltimore, MD: Johns Hopkins University Press, 1998), 12.

3 For a history of this subordination, see Thomas Nail, *Being and Motion* (Oxford: Oxford University Press, 2019).

4 Aristotle, *Metaphysics*, 1029a20. My translation.

5 Ibid., 1007b27-28. See also ibid., Gamma, sections 4–6. Note that not all philosophies of indeterminacy are materialist.

6 Emanuela Bianchi, *The Feminine Symptom: Aleatory Matter in the Aristotelian Cosmos* (New York: Fordham University Press, 2014).

7 On the similarities and differences of usage of Plato's *chora* and Aristotle's *hûlē*, see Dennis Polis, 'A New Reading of Aristotle's "Hyle"', *Modern Schoolman* 68, no. 3 (1991): 225–44. See also John Sallis, *Chorology: On Beginning in Plato's Timaeus* (Bloomington: Indiana University Press, 2020), 151.

8 Henry George Liddell and Robert Scott, *A Greek–English Lexicon*, revised and augmented throughout by Sir Henry Stuart Jones, with the assistance of Roderick McKenzie (Oxford: Clarendon Press, 1940).

9 Plato, *Timaeus*, 52E.

10 David Asheri, *Distribuzioni di terre nelle antica Grecia* (Turin: Memorie dell'Accademia delle Scienze di Torino, 1966), 10.

11 Thanos Zartaloudis, *The Birth of Nomos* (Edinburgh: Edinburgh University Press, 2020), xxvi.

12 Asheri, *Distribuzioni di terre*, 14.

13 Emmanuel Laroche, *Histoire de la racine NEM- en grec ancien* (Paris: Klincksieck, 1949), 116.

14 Ibid., 255.

15 Ibid., 116.

16 See Zartaloudis, *The Birth of Nomos*, xx–xxviii.

17 Maria Theodorou, 'Space as Experience: "Chore/Choros"', *Architectural Association School of Architecture* 34 (autumn 1997): 45–55 (54).

18 John Chadwick, *The Decipherment of Linear B*, 2nd edn (Cambridge: Cambridge University Press, 2014), 134.

19 Anne Baring and Jules Cashford, *The Myth of the Goddess: Evolution of an Image* (London: Arkana, 2000), 108.

20 For an account of the transition and possible influence of the Minoans on the later Greeks, see the first three chapters of Carl Kerenyi, *Dionysos: Archetypal Image of Indestructible Life*, trans. Ralph Manheim (Princeton, NJ: Princeton University Press, 1976). For three specific examples of this influence I have chosen the cult of Dodona, the Eleusinian mysteries and the oracle of Delphi.

21 For description of these 'cult places', see Nanno Marinatos, *Minoan Religion: Ritual, Image and Symbol* (Columbia, SC: University of South Carolina Press, 1993); Bogdan Rutkowski, *The Cult Places of the Aegean* (New Haven, CT: Yale University Press, 1986); and Livingston V. Watrous, *The Cave Sanctuary of Zeus at Psychro: A Study of Extra-Urban Sanctuaries in Minoan and Early Iron Age Crete* (Liège and Austin, TX: Université de Liège and University of Texas at Austin, 1996). For a survey of the locations of these extra-urban ritual locations, see Elissa Faro, 'Ritual Activity and Regional Dynamics: Towards a Reinterpretation of Minoan Extra-Urban Ritual Space', PhD dissertation, University of Michigan, 2008.

22 Caroline Tully and Sam Crooks, 'Dropping Ecstasy? Minoan Cult and the Tropes of Shamanism', *Time and Mind: The Journal of Archaeology, Consciousness and Culture* 8, no. 2 (2015): 129–58.

23 Robert B. Koehl, 'The Ambiguity of the Minoan Mind', in Eva Alram-Stern, Fritz Blakolmer, Sigrid Deger-Jalkotzy, Robert Laffineur and Jörg Weilhartner (eds), *Metaphysis: Ritual, Myth and Symbolism in the*

Aegean Bronze Age. 15th International Aegean Conference, University of Vienna, 22–25 April 2014 (Leuven: Peeters, 2016), 470.

24 Some Minoan images depict floating figures, but these may be depictions of ecstatic visions and not necessarily particular transcendent gods from other worlds. See Caroline Tully, 'Virtual Reality: Tree Cult and Epiphanic Ritual in Aegean Glyptic Iconography', *Journal of Prehistoric Religion* 25 (2016): 19–30; and Vesa-Pekka Herva, 'Flower Lovers, After All? Rethinking Religion and Human–Environment Relations in Minoan Crete', *World Archaeology* 38, no. 4 (2006): 586–98.

25 Koehl, 'Ambiguity of the Minoan Mind', 470.

26 Ibid., 470–2.

27 Ibid.

28 Ibid.

29 Ibid.

30 See Figures 15, 16, 17 and 18 in Tully and Crooks, 'Dropping Ecstasy?', 143–5.

31 See Figure 19 in ibid., 145.

32 See the seal impression from Zakros in Marija Gimbutas, *The Gods and Goddesses of Old Europe, 7000 to 3500 BC: Myths, Legends and Cult Images* (Berkeley: University of California Press, 1974), 186.

33 See Figures 20, 21, 22, and 23 in Tully and Crooks, 'Dropping Ecstasy?', 146–8.

34 Tully and Crooks, 'Dropping Ecstasy?', 145.

35 See Anna Simandiraki-Grimshaw, 'Minoan Animal–Human Hybridity', in D. B. Counts and B. Arnold (eds), *The Master of Animals in Old World Iconography* (Budapest: Archaeolingua Alapítvány, 2010), 96.

36 Koehl, 'Ambiguity of the Minoan Mind', 470–2.

37 Ibid.

38 Ibid.

39 Herva, 'Flower Lovers, After All?' 588.

40 For a resonant approach to thinking about 'persons' and non-human agencies, see Tim Ingold, *Perception of the Environment: Essays on Livelihood, Dwelling and Skill* (Abingdon: Routledge, 2021), 90–8. For an example of the 'new animism' approach, see Graham Harvey, *Animism: Respecting the Living World* (London: Hurst, 2005), 99–114.

41 For an excellent introduction to the idea of 'new animism', the critique of modernist understandings of animism, and a case study of environmental agency in the Nayaka hunter-gatherers in South India, see Nurit Bird-David, '"Animism" Revisited: Personhood, Environment and Relational Epistemology', *Current*

Anthropology: A World Journal of the Sciences of Man 40, no. S1 (1999), esp. pp. 74–5.

42 Herva, 'Flower Lovers, After All?'

43 Rod Barnett, 'Sacred Groves: Sacrifice and the Order of Nature in Ancient Greek Landscapes', *Landscape Journal* 26, no. 2 (2007): 252–69; see 256 for discussion and debate.

44 Vincent Scully, *The Earth, the Temple, and the Gods: Greek Sacred Architecture* (New Haven, CT: Yale University Press, 1979), 89.

45 Scholars seem to agree that cult activity began some time between the late Bronze Age and early Iron Age. 'Objects and archaeological remains at the site of Dodona suggest that there was already some kind of cult activity there in the late Bronze Age': Esther Eidinow, 'Oracles and Oracle-Sellers. An Ancient Market in Futures', in David Engles and Peter Van Nuffelen (eds), *Religion and Competition in Antiquity* (Brussels: Éditions Latomus, 2014), 63, citing S. Dakaris, Ανασκαφη του ιερου της Δωδωνης in PAE (1967), 33–54, at 39f. 'From the Early Iron Age … the first unquestionable evidence of cult activity is detected': Jessica Piccinini, *The Shrine of Dodona in the Archaic and Classical Ages: A History* (Macerata: EUM, 2017), 41.

46 See Piccinini, *The Shrine of Dodona*, 25. n. 24. See also H. W. Parke, *The Oracles of Zeus: Dodona, Olympia, Ammon* (Cambridge, MA: Harvard University Press, 1967), 68, 78, n. 36. According to Strabo (VII, 7, 12, C 329), at a certain point the cult was established at Dodona and the goddess became a temple-associate of Zeus. Herbert Parke writes that 'It is much more likely that the alleged introduction of Dione is a scholarly hypothesis and that, instead, as most modern scholars would suppose, she had been present at Dodona as Zeus's female consort since time immemorial … Of course another possibility must be reckoned with. The cult of Dione might have been primeval at Dodona, but at some period in the dark ages it might have risen in importance from being subordinate to Zeus until in the end it was dominant enough to have dictated the sex of the chief officials in the temple. This is not exactly what Strabo says, but one might argue that it was a more correct description of what actually happened. However, here again one must observe that Herodotus, our first evidence for the priestesses, and a man who had actually interviewed them, treats Dodona as a shrine and oracle of Zeus, and never mentions Dione at all. Again the inscriptions from Dodona itself confirm this picture. They mention or are addressed to Zeus Naios, either alone or often in conjunction with Dione. But Zeus always leads, if both are mentioned, and it is very rare for Zeus to be omitted, and Dione named alone.' Parke, *The Oracles of Zeus*, 69–70.

47 The tree shaking depicted in Minoan artefacts may have been used at Dodona. According to Tully, 'Tree-shaking may have produced a sound utilised for divination, as did Zeus' oak at Dodona.' Caroline Tully, 'The Sacred Life of Trees: What Trees Say about People in the Prehistoric Aegean and Near East', *News from the Australian Society for Classical Studies*, https://www.ascs.org.au/news/ascs33/TULLY. pdf, p. 3 (accessed 28 April 2023). For a more detailed treatment of Aegean tree cults, see Caroline J. Tully, *The Cultic Life of Trees in the Prehistoric Aegean, Levant, Egypt and Cyprus* (Leuven: Peeters, 2018).

48 D. M. Nicol, 'The Oracle of Dodona', *Greece & Rome* 5, no. 2 (1958): 143.

49 Walter Burkert, *Greek Religion: Archaic and Classical*, trans. John Raffan (Cambridge, MA: Harvard University Press, 1985), 85.

50 Scully, *The Earth, the Temple, and the Gods*, 1.

51 Hesiod, *Theogony & Words and Days*, trans. Richard Caldwell, ed. Stephanie Nelson (Indianapolis: Hackett, 2015), line 887.

52 Michael Simpson, '"Odyssey 9": Symmetry and Paradox in Outis', *The Classical Journal* 68, no. 1 (1972): 22–5.

53 For a collection of essays on trickster figures in mythology, see William J. Hynes and William G. Doty, *Mythical Trickster Figures: Contours, Contexts and Criticisms* (Tuscaloosa: University of Alabama Press, 1993).

54 ἴδη in Henry Liddell and Robert Scott, *Greek-English Lexicon* (Oxford: Clarendon Press, 1940).

55 Gregory Nagy, 'Greek-Like Elements in Linear A', *Greek, Roman, and Byzantine Studies* 4, no. 200 (1963): 200.

56 Hesiod, *Theogony*, 477–84.

57 Ibid., 116.

58 Robert Mondi, 'Χαος and the Hesiodic Cosmogony Author(s)', *Harvard Studies in Classical Philology* 92 (1989): 1–41.

59 Watkins Calvert, *The American Heritage Dictionary of Proto-Indo-European Roots*, 2nd edn (Boston: Houghton Mifflin, 2000), 32.

60 '"First of all", says Hesiod, "Chaos came into being"—What does that mean? "Chaos" was not at first, as we conceive it, formless disorder. The word means simply the "Yawning gap"—the gap we now see, with its lower part filled with air and mist and cloud, between earth and the dome of heaven.' Francis Cornford, *From Religion to Philosophy: A Study of the Origins of Western Speculation* (Princeton, NJ: Princeton University Press, 2009 [1912]), 66–7. 'Although the flaws in Cornford's arguments are obvious, his position is repeated, either directly or in a modified stance, in influential works from Geoffrey

Kirk, John Raven and Malcolm Schofield's *The Presocratic Philosophers: A Critical History with a Selection of Texts*, 2nd edn (Cambridge: Cambridge University Press, 1983), p. 33, right up to Andrew Gregory's *Ancient Greek Cosmogony* (London: Bristol Classical Press, 2007), p. 23. The Chaos-as-gap reading has become so influential that some important translations even replace Hesiod's first god with a more neutral term, such as Chasm. See Martin West (ed. and trans.), *Hesiod's Theogony* (Oxford: Oxford University Press, 1999). Indeed, even in studies critical of Cornford's specific position, his gap remains a symptom of something more pervasive, and the vast majority of the *Theogony*'s interpreters agree that not only was Hesiod describing an ordered cosmological account, but that his poem constitutes a pivotal first step towards the rational cosmologies of the later Greek philosophers such as the Milesian monists. See Jenny Clay, *Hesiod's Cosmos* (Cambridge: Cambridge University Press, 2003). Clay, in her sophisticated reading of the poem, does not interpret Chaos as a gap. Nevertheless, she is careful to distance it from disorder, noting "this is apparently not, as we might think, a jumble of undifferentiated matter, but rather its negation, a featureless void" (*Hesiod's Cosmos*, 15). From this starting point, her reading, following a generally Milesian pattern, searches for the underlying order in Hesiod's poem.' Almqvist Olaf, 'Hesiod's *Theogony* and Analogist Cosmogonies', *HAU: Journal of Ethnographic Theory* 10, no. 1 (2020): 187–8.

61 Michael Puett, 'Social Order or Social Chaos', in Robert Orsi (ed.), *The Cambridge Companion to Religious Studies* (Cambridge: Cambridge University Press, 2011), 109–29; Michael Scott, *The Severed Snake: Matrilineages, Making Place, and a Melanesian Christianity in Southeast Solomon Islands* (Durham, NC: Carolina Academic Press, 2007).

62 Mondi, 'Χαοσ and the Hesiodic Cosmogony Author(s)', 7.

63 Chantraine and Pokorny list them under separate cross-referenced entries. For the IE root *gheu-, see J. Pokorny, *Indogermanisches etymologisches Worterbuch* (Bern, 1948–69), 449; P. Chantraine, *Dictionnaire etymologique de la langue grecque* (Paris, 1968–80), 1239–40.

64 H. Frisk, *Griechisches etymologisches Worterbuch* (Heidelberg: Universitätsverlag Winter, 1961–72), 1073.

65 Mondi, 'Χαοσ and the Hesiodic Cosmogony Author(s)', 8

66 See Thomas Nail, *The Birth of Chaos*, ch. 4, unpublished MS.

67 Hesiod, *Theogony*, line 728.

68 Giovanni Cerri, 'The Concept of "Matter" in Archaic Greece, 1: Khaos/Aèr in Hesiod's Theogony', *Peitho. Examina Antiqua* 8, no. 1 (2017): 53–80.

69 'To this extent Tartarus represents, in spatial terms, what Chaos does in temporal ones: the primordial indeterminacy from which the world will later be organised into regions and differentiated cosmic elements.' Marcel Detienne and Jean-Pierre Vernant, *Cunning Intelligence in Greek Culture and Society*, trans. Janet Lloyd (Chicago: University of Chicago Press, 1991), 169.

70 M. L. West (ed.), *Hesiod: Theogony* (Oxford: Clarendon Press, 1966), 361.

71 See Homer, *Iliad* 23.127, 'ἄσπετον ὕλην'; 'ἄσπετον ὕλην', *Iliad* 24.784; 'ἄσπετον ὕλην', *Iliad* 2.455, 'just as a fire makes a boundless forest blaze on the peaks of a mountain' (my translation). See also Homer, 'Hymn to Dionysus', line 10: 'ἄσπετον ὕλην'.

72 Aristotle, *Physics: Books 1–4*, trans. P. H. Wicksteed and F. M. Cornford (Cambridge, MA: Harvard University Press, 1957), Book IV, lines 1208b25–27.

73 Although the two words are probably not etymologically related, they share very similar usage in Hesiod and Plato. There is also an affinity with the originary Hesiodic chaos, or gap, as alluded to by Derrida and explicitly noted by Nader El-Bizri in his essay on *chōra*. Jacques Derrida, 'Chora', trans. Ian McCloud, in *Chora L Works: Jacques Derrida and Peter Eisenman*, ed. Jeffrey Kipnis and Thomas Leeser (New York: The Monacelli Press, 1997), 15–32 (21); Nader El-Bizri, '"Qui etes-vous Chōra?" Receiving Plato's Timaeus', *Existentia* 11 (2001): 473–90 (475). 'The reading and analysis of the feminine receptacle/*chōra* as restless, errant, and indeterminate suggests that it may be a potentially useful theoretical locus through which to reread and perhaps displace the metaphysical architecture handed down to us by Plato and Aristotle.' Bianchi, *The Feminine Symptom*, 101. See also John Bussanich, 'A Theoretical Interpretation of Hesiod's Chaos', *Classical Philology* 78, no. 3 (1983): 212–19. 'Plotinus uses the word chaos only once, taking it as a sort of container, like Timaeus, into which the divine (forms) are inserted. The word Χάος comes from χαόω, swallow up (cf. also χαινω and χασκω); it is, thus, what is gaping (like the jaws of a crocodile), a yawning chasm (hence its association with space); it is the nether abyss, infinite darkness.' George Seidel, 'Chaos in Plotinus', *Revue de Philosophie Ancienne* 10, no. 2 (1992): 211–20. See also Laura Gemelli, 'Chaos Chora: An Academic Interpretation of Hesiod', *Aristoteles bis zum Neuplatonismus, Prometheus* 17 (1991): 218–34. 'Hesiod's view of the order of being, then, is both indeterminate in its inception and precarious in its stability, both incentives to differentiating thinkers to come to more definitively establish being and more clearly distinguish it from becoming and

non-being.' Richard Moorton, 'Hesiod as Precursor to the Presocratic Philosophers: A Voeglinian View' (2001), 5, https://sites01.lsu.edu/faculty/voegelin/wp-content/uploads/sites/80/2015/09/Moorton.pdf (accessed 28 April 2023). See also Arum Park, 'Parthenogenesis in Hesiod's Theogony', *Preternature: Critical and Historical Studies on the Preternatural* 3, no. 2 (2014): 261–83.

74 Robert Pogue Harrison, *Forests: The Shadow of Civilization* (Chicago: University of Chicago Press, 1992), x.

75 However, most ancient and modern commentators read Lucretius as having added nothing to Epicurus' philosophy and not diverged from it in any way. I find this idea of radical fundamentalism difficult to accept for many reasons. See Thomas Nail, *Lucretius I: An Ontology of Motion* (Edinburgh: Edinburgh University Press, 2018); Thomas Nail, *Lucretius II: An Ethics of Motion* (Edinburgh: Edinburgh University Press, 2020); and Thomas Nail, *Lucretius III: A History of Motion* (Edinburgh: Edinburgh University Press, 2022).

76 After Homer and Hesiod, the idea of *material indeterminacy* in the kinetic materialist tradition passed through the early Greek and classical philosophers without any full adherents until the Roman poet Lucretius in the first century BCE. I cannot show how every ancient author rejected the postulates of kinetic materialism here, but I have done so in *Being and Motion* (Oxford: Oxford University Press, 2019).

77 Although he does use the word *particula* to describe particles of images (4.775), food, mind (3.708) and wind (4.260), he does not use it to describe the nature of matter.

78 Pierre Vesperini, *Lucrèce: Archéologie d'un classique européen* (Paris: Fayard, 2017). Even Epicurus only uses the adjective ἄτομ-, meaning 'indivisible', 51 times. Epicurus also uses the noun σῶμα, meaning body, 53 times. This indicates that Epicurus may not have had such a discrete idea of matter either.

79 See Nail, *Lucretius I*; Nail, *Lucretius II*; and Nail, *Lucretius III*.

80 Titus Lucretius Carus, *De Rerum Natura (On the Nature of Things)*, ed. Walter Englert (Newburyport, MA: Focus Publishing, 2003), 1.966–7. My translation.

81 Ibid., 5.436.

82 Marcello Gigante, *Philodemus in Italy: The Books from Herculaneum*, trans. Dirk Obbink (Ann Arbor, MI: University of Michigan Press, 1995), 42.

83 For a nice account of indirect evidence, see Tim O'Keefe, 'Does Epicurus Need the Swerve as an Archê of Collisions?', *Phronesis* 41, no. 3 (1996): 305–17.

84 Lucretius, *De Rerum Natura*, 2.221 [*solerent*]; 2.244–5.

85 For example, the French philosopher Gilles Deleuze explicitly subordinates matter and motion to *force* in his reading of Lucretius. Gilles Deleuze, *Nietzsche and Philosophy* (New York: Columbia University Press, 1983), 6–7. See also Gilles Deleuze, *Logic of Sense*, trans. Mark Lester and Charles Stivale (New York: Columbia University Press, 1990), 266–79. We might also include process philosophers such as Henri Bergson and Alfred North Whitehead, who disagreed with Lucretius' idea that matter moved indeterminately on its own. The influence of these thinkers on contemporary philosophy has been extremely important. For a survey of some of the debates, see Adrian Ivakhiv, 'Beatnik Brothers? Between Graham Harman and the Deleuzo-Whiteheadian Axis', *Parrhesia* 19 (2014): 65–78.

86 Lucretius, *De Rerum Natura*, 2.218–20.

87 Ibid., 2.219 [*depellere*].

88 Ibid., 2.220 [*momen mutatum*].

89 Ibid., 2.119 [*paulum*].

90 Ibid., 2.218–19.

Chapter 2

Modern Indeterminacy: Marx's Void, Woolf's Moments and Quantum Flux

In this chapter I show how Lucretius transmitted the notion of indeterminate materialism from the Archaic Greek poets to modern thinkers of indeterminate materialism. Unfortunately, most ancient and modern readers found Lucretius' idea of a material and indeterminate swerve philosophically unpalatable. How could matter move without something else moving it? They tended to prefer a world of deterministic atoms created by God, following natural laws, and manipulated by rational humans with immortal souls.[1]

Karl Marx and Virginia Woolf were very close readers of Lucretius and got their theories of indeterminacy explicitly and directly from him. Unlike many others who read Lucretius, Marx and Woolf did not think of the swerve as occasional, or happening *in* space and time, caused by something else such as vital force, or made of discrete atoms.[2] They thought of matter and motion as 'indeterminate relational processes', as I define those terms in this book. More recently, many contemporary physicists have admitted what early modern European scientists refused to admit: that Lucretius was right about the indeterminacy of matter. This is the story I want to tell in this chapter.

Marx's Void

The first modern author to fully affirm the indeterminacy of Lucretius' kinetic materialism was the young German philosopher Karl Marx, writing in the nineteenth century. Long before Marx had read any of the great German philosopher Friedrich Hegel's writing, he was a poet and close reader of Lucretius. Marx's first philosophical passion was to critique religion and propose a new theory of materialism. After reading Hegel, Marx wrote his doctoral dissertation blending ancient materialism with Hegel's dialectical philosophy to create something new: a *swerving* dialectical materialism.

Although the title of Marx's dissertation was about the difference between Epicurus and his teacher Democritus, Marx cited Lucretius' poem as many times as Epicurus' three short letters preserved by Diogenes. Additionally, Marx dedicated two of his seven dissertation notebooks to close readings and translations of Lucretius' poem. If we include these notebooks, Marx spent more time directly engaging with Lucretius' poem than with Epicurus' primary texts. Lucretius, Marx said, was 'the only one in general of all the ancients who has understood Epicurean physics'.[3] Whatever Marx thought about the similarities and differences between Epicurus and Lucretius, the fact remains that everything Marx or any of his sources knew about the swerve came from Lucretius' poem, *not* from Epicurus.

The most radical aspect of Marx's materialism was his realisation that if everything is material, and if matter is 'the cause of everything, [then matter is] without cause itself'; it must be immanently self-caused.[4] Marx was also one of the few readers who affirmed the radical indeterminacy of the swerve and the primacy of motion in Lucretius.[5]

For instance, Marx wrote that 'This *declinatio*, this *clinamen* [declination, deviation], is neither *regione loci certa* nor *tempore certo* [defined by place, determined by time] ... That is, it is no external condition of motion, but being-for-self, immanent, absolute movement itself.'[6] This idea of material kinetic indeterminacy without external cause is the fundamental idea that makes Marx's materialism a genuine successor to Lucretius.

Furthermore, one of Marx's great contributions to reading Epicurus was that he interpreted the void, the atom, its fall and its swerve as inseparable aspects of the *same* indeterminate material process – not as discrete things. Marx wrote that 'The consequence of this for ... the atoms would therefore be – since they are in constant motion – that [they do not] exist but rather disappear in the straight line; for the solidity of the atom does not even enter into the picture.'[7] One can hardly imagine a more radical departure from the atomist tradition than to say, as Marx does here, that *as a process*, 'atoms do not exist!' There is no discrete or ontologically different substance called an eternal atom. The atom is only an abstract moment in the dialectical unfolding of matter. Furthermore, if motion is indeterminate, there is no determinate atom separate from any other.

Similarly, Marx wrote that 'the void, the negation, is not the negative of matter itself'.[8] The void is made through the movement of indeterminate matter just as *khaos* and *chora* were.[9] In this way, Marx completely reinterpreted the Epicurean and Democritean dualism between atom and void as a 'material dialectic' of folding and unfolding. Atoms emerge or unfold out of the void, which 'holds its ground'.[10]

Matters move beyond and yet always unfold from previous ones. In his dissertation, Marx understood the 'materialist dialectic' as an *indeterminate* relational process. He also interpreted Epicurus' theory of time as a theory of indeterminate change more generally. 'The *accidens* is the change of substance in general. The *accidens* of the *accidens* is the change as reflecting in itself, the change as change.'[11] In other words, for Marx, matter and motion is not a change in an underlying substance, but *the change of change* itself: absolute indeterminate movement.

Marx was not only trying to explicate Epicurus but was trying to use his explication to develop a materialist dialectic contra Hegel's idealist dialectic. And ultimately, the indeterminate swerve of matter was the key difference between Marx's dialectical philosophy and Hegel's. In his later economic and political writings, Marx argued that the core philosophical problem with capitalism was that it treats nature as if it were a bunch of determinate and discrete objects with economic 'value'. However, according to Marx's interpretation of Epicurus and Lucretius, there are no fixed physical entities, no fixed values, and no fixed relations between physical entities and units of value. In this way, for Marx, capitalism is fundamentally wrong as a description of the world.

Capitalism treats the world as an 'immense collection of commodities; the individual commodity being its elementary form'.[12] Capitalism treats the diverse and changing world of natural processes as if it were discrete exchangeable units of what Marx called economic 'value'. In this way, Marx explicitly compared his critique of the commodity with his earlier critique of the 'abstract individuality and self-sufficiency' of atoms in Democritus' materialism.[13]

For Marx, capitalism also assumes that the 'value form' is superior and independent from what Marx called 'use-values' or the 'material bearers' (*Träger*) of value. Use-values are the sensuous qualities of things being used.

But capitalism treats things as abstract quantities as if they had no qualities or use-values. Capitalists invented the idea of abstract quantitative value by exploiting the qualitative aspects of nature, women, slaves and workers, and then pretending that these processes were reducible to a quantity of economic value. This economic reduction has tended to exploit some groups more than others, following a specific Euro-Western hierarchy.[14] Capitalism is another historical instance where *form* (as quantitative value) is treated as superior to the constant qualitative flux of *matter*.[15]

By contrast, Marx argued in his dissertation that nature is indeterminate processes. There are no pre-given hierarchies or discrete units. In this way, capitalism is a dangerous delusion about the nature of things. For Marx, many kinds of ethical and political behaviour could be consistent with the idea of natural indeterminacy, but fixed hierarchies and capitalism are not.

This is why Marx did not describe communism as a single fixed social plan. Marx intended communism to be an open social arrangement whereby people experimented and adapted to their changing circumstances like swerves of matter. In particular, Marx thought that if everyone shared in maintaining collective subsistence they could maximise their free time to 'go dancing, go drinking, think, love, theorize, sing, paint, fence, etc.'[16] People rarely emphasise Marx's definition of communism as the 'emancipation of all human senses and attributes',[17] but this idea is directly related to his theory of sensation in his dissertation.[18] For Marx, communism is possible only because nature is indeterminate and open to all kinds of yet-unimagined social-aesthetic sensations without any formal hierarchy above matter.[19] Marx knew that communism did not guarantee the good life, but was the ongoing struggle to do so.

Woolf's Moments of Being Indeterminate

The twentieth-century English novelist Virginia Woolf also read Lucretius' *De Rerum Natura* many times throughout her life, annotated it, and translated many of its most important passages.[20] Like Marx, her conclusions were extremely heterodox compared to those of her contemporaries. Woolf described how the fall and swerve of atoms disappeared entirely into the patterns of everyday life.

The task of art and modern literature in particular, for Woolf, was not to describe the objective external world of things or the subjective inner world of thoughts and feelings. The challenge, for Woolf, was to articulate their *indeterminate flux*. In her famous short essay, 'Modern Fiction', Woolf wrote:

> From all sides they come, an incessant shower of innumerable atoms; and as they fall, as they shape themselves into the life of Monday or Tuesday, the accent falls differently from of old; the moment of importance came not here but there.[21]

Modern writing's challenge is to record the patterns traced by the indeterminate swerve, however hybrid, metamorphic and incoherent. Like Marx, these swerving atoms disappear entirely into unpredictable patterns of motion. Woolf writes, 'Let us record the atoms as they fall upon the mind in the order in which they fall, let us trace the pattern, however disconnected and incoherent in appearance.'[22]

So, although Marx and Woolf both use the term 'atom', when Lucretius did not, they both think of it as an indeterminate movement without an external cause such as God. They both treat its movement in non-discrete ways, either dialectically or in terms of patterns. This comes out explicitly when the characters in Woolf's novels occasionally catch glimpses of explicitly indeterminate processes through what Woolf called 'moments of being'.[23]

For example, in Woolf's novel *Mrs. Dalloway* (1925), Clarissa Dalloway stops at the gates of a park on her walk to buy flowers and stands for a moment watching the omnibuses circulate through Piccadilly Square. Suddenly, the shocking sight of vast masses of people, buses and taxis moving along the crowded street fills her with an overwhelming sensation of movement. She begins to feel part of a larger flow in the city, on the earth, in the cosmos.

But this is odd because to feel one's being as a process within a process is not a discrete total state that one can easily conceptualise. Motion is not a state of being but a moment of becoming. While in motion, Mrs Dalloway feels one is never fully present or identical to one's self. Woolf writes that 'To her [Mrs Dalloway] it was absolutely absorbing; all this; the cabs passing; and she would not say of Peter, she would not say of herself, I am this, I am that … She would not say of any one in the world now that they were this or were that.'[24] As a process, Mrs Dalloway feels the loss of her identity and becomes *indeterminate*.

Woolf's rejection of a higher explanation for the swerve of matter is explicit in her posthumously published autobiography *Moments of Being*. There she wrote that

> the whole world is a work of art; that we are parts of the work of art … There is no Shakespeare, there is no Beethoven; certainly and emphatically there is no God; we are the words; we are the music; we are the thing itself. And I see this when I have a shock.[25]

There is no ontological division between nature and culture for Woolf. The artist is not separate from nature but performs its indeterminacy through creativity.

From this we can surmise that if we are nature and we are 'neither this nor that', then nature is also 'neither this nor that'.[26] Indeed, Mrs Dalloway describes this indeterminacy as the feeling of 'slicing like a knife through everything'[27] or being a formless mist.

> Somehow in the streets of London, on the ebb and flow of things, here, there, she survived, Peter survived, lived in each other, she being part, she was positive, of the trees at home; of the house there, ugly, rambling all to bits and pieces as it was; part of people she had never met; being laid out like a mist between the people she knew best, who lifted her on their branches as she had seen the trees lift the mist, but it spread ever so far, her life, herself.[28]

Mrs Dalloway feels like a shapeless mist floating through the indeterminate forest of the world.

> But she said, sitting on the bus going up Shaftesbury Avenue, she felt herself everywhere; not 'here, here, here'; and she tapped the back of the seat; but everywhere. She waved her hand, going up Shaftesbury Avenue. She was all that. So that to know her, or any one, one must seek out the people who completed them; even the places. Odd affinities she had with people she had never spoken to, some woman in the street, some man behind a counter – even trees, or barns.[29]

When Mrs Dalloway is in motion, she feels that she has no determinate being in space or time, just like Lucretius' swerve. She is neither here *nor* there because she is in process. The logic of contradiction breaks down in these moments. '[Mrs Dalloway] felt very young; at the same time unspeakably aged.'[30]

Let's look at one of many more possible examples. In Woolf's novel *Orlando* (1928), the main character Orlando takes a long drive. She begins to feel that 'everything was partly something else, and each gained an odd moving power from this union of itself and something not itself so that with this mixture of truth and falsehood her mind became like a forest in which things moved; lights and shadows changed, and one thing became another'.[31] Woolf's description here of the forest's hybridity and indeterminacy echoes the archaic image of the formless and indeterminate forest where movement and metamorphosis were ritually experienced. When Orlando feels herself becoming a process, the world becomes a moving and indeterminate mixture of self and other, true and false.

For Woolf, material processes have no logical contradictions because they are not about determinate beings. Reality is like a wave, Woolf writes: 'It was Yes, No. Yes, yes, yes, the tide rushed out embracing. No, no, no, it contracted.'[32] Bernard, a character from Woolf's novel *The Waves* (1931), says, 'There is no stability in this world … To speak of knowledge is futile. All is experiment and adventure. We are forever mixing ourselves with unknown quantities. What is to come? I know not.'[33]

Woolf also drew her own aesthetic and political consequences from these Lucretian moments of indeterminacy. Her moments of being were not objective metaphysical visions of *all* reality. Instead, they were more intense ranges of sensation than usual. Their function, for Woolf, was to show us that metaphysics, idealism and transcendent values and forms are all illusions. There is no God, no sin, no lack, no hierarchy of beings, no judgement, no justification for patriarchy, and no reason to fear death – just as Lucretius had said. Woolf's moments of being remind us that all seemingly immutable forms are only patterns open to swerving experimentation.

In this way, the 'moment of vision' for Woolf and Lucretius strongly impressed upon the visionary the falseness and absurdity of ontological discreteness. Indeed, living as if the world were discrete objects that are here for our use is a dangerous idea, which Marx critiqued as 'atomistic' commodification. For Woolf, art and sensation can bring us to these conclusions just as well as philosophy.[34]

This is why Woolf thought moments of being should be socially protected, facilitated and made available to everyone through socialism. Social, economic and physical safety gives people space and time to explore unique moments of indeterminacy. In *A Room of One's Own*, Woolf argued that we all, especially women, need a room of our own and a guaranteed livable income. Moments of being do not require special education, but as material states, certain situations can help or hinder them. In short, Woolf strongly believed that patriarchy, capitalism and imperialism hindered art and moments of being indeterminate. Instead, she imagined socialism and feminism as capable of supporting aesthetic experiences of indeterminacy for everyone.[35]

Quantum Fluctuations

Contemporary quantum physicists have also been reading Lucretius. Many now admit that Lucretius was the first to conceptualise quantum indeterminacy with his idea of the swerve. The Italian quantum physicist Carlo Rovelli writes that 'quantum events, the individual events at the basis of modern physics, happen randomly ... which, in Lucretius' marvelous verses, happen "*incerto tempore ... incertisque locis*": at a random time and in a random place'.[36] The English word 'random' is not a good translation of the Latin word *incerto* here, but Rovelli's credit to Lucretius is important. The American quantum physicist Sean Carroll has also written that 'Lucretius proposes that the universe arises as a quantum fluctuation.'[37]

Other physicists have directly compared Lucretius' swerve to Heisenberg's quantum uncertainty principle.[38] 'Lucretius' swerve results in the same kind of uncertainty that Heisenberg's principle requires', writes physicist Brian Dodson.[39] Classical scholars of Lucretius also tend to agree with this quantum interpretation.[40] Even the well-known Lucretius scholar David Sedley writes that the swerve has 'a striking resemblance to the indeterminacy postulated by modern quantum physics'.[41]

Quantum indeterminacy is an important experimental result of contemporary physics, although many physicists are not happy about it. When they can, they try to 'renormalise' its noisy effects and use probabilistic equations to make educated guesses about indeterminate quantum behaviours. Some have even come up with interpretations of quantum mechanics that try to *explain away* quantum indeterminacy as the effect of 'hidden deterministic variables' or 'alternate universes' that we have not yet discovered.[42] Despite probabilistic equations and speculative metaphysical theories of determinism, indeterminacy persists as an experimental result that physicists cannot interpret away. Here we should look to the less metaphysically burdened work of Carlo Rovelli.[43]

What is quantum indeterminacy? Quantum fields are the underlying distributions of energy in the universe. They are not made of anything else that we know of, nor are they objects in any classical or relativistic sense. They are not in a single place, nor do they have any fixed properties. We cannot even observe them directly. We can only record the *traces* of their interactions left on our measuring instruments.[44]

The lowest energy state of these quantum fields is called the 'vacuum'. However, the energy of the vacuum is not zero. The vacuum is not static but instead fluctuates indeterminately without necessarily producing any observable or determinate particles.[45] The American physicist Karen Barad writes that 'the vacuum is not (determinately) empty, nor is it (determinately) not empty'. Instead, it has 'indeterminacies–in–action ... [that] do not exist in space and time ... In/determinacy is not the state of a thing but an unending dynamism.'[46] Significantly, this is why Barad compares the quantum vacuum with Archaic cosmologies similar to Hesiod's, where 'Nature is birthed out of chaos and void ... out of a fecund nothingness.'[47]

The nature of these quantum vacuum fluctuations is perhaps the single greatest mystery and challenge facing cosmology and fundamental physics today. They are at the heart of every known object as well as the dark energies accelerating our universe.[48] Dark energy is nothing other than the quantum vacuum fluctuations that collectively pull our universe in all directions. From the quantum to the cosmic, these vacuum fluctuations are the vast, invisible *engines of nature*. In other words, the most revolutionary discovery of contemporary physics is that our universe is not reducible to determinate self–identical objects as we have ever understood them. *Energy is indeterminate.*

Although we tend to associate the term 'vacuum' with void or emptiness, the opposite is the case in quantum physics. 'A quantum field implies that its vacuum is a humming hive of activity. Fluctuations continually take place, in the course of which transient "particles" appear and disappear.

A quantum vacuum is more like a plenum than like empty space', writes English physicist John Polkinghorne.[49] Particles do not float in an empty void. The English physicist Frank Close comments,

> A vacuum is not empty but seethes with transient particles of matter and antimatter, which bubble in and out of existence. Although these will-o'-the-wisps are invisible to our normal senses, they disturb the photon and electron in the moment of their union and contribute to the number that the experiment measures.[50]

Physicists call these transient particles 'virtual particles' even though they are neither virtual nor particles – but rather *kinetic vibrations* of energy.

Physicists describe the motion of these fluctuations as 'turbulent whirlpools' and their effect on the equations of quantum field theory as 'perturbation theories'. What experimental physicists interpret as the electron's finite mass is, in fact, the result of the emergent pattern of indeterminate motions in a whole region of a field's vacuum that fills the creative/destructive void.[51]

But vacuum fluctuations do not only 'perturb' particles; particles *are* excitations in the fields. In quantum field theory, all matter is fluctuations that originate in the vacuum and continue to perturb the stability of observable particles. For instance, most of the mass of protons and neutrons is not due to their quarks, which make up only 1 per cent of their mass, but the result of the *movements* of the indeterminate vacuum fluctuations within them.[52]

Quantum fluctuations are not processes or changes *of* a substance but the *accidens* of the *accidens*, or 'absolute movement', as Marx wrote. Quantum fluctuations also exhibit a fundamental 'uncertainty ... in or between two states of existence', similar to Minoan notions of ambiguity. In its own way, and perhaps without knowing the extent of it, the science of quantum fluctuations continues the tradition of indeterminate materialism.[53]

But how are all these indeterminate processes related to one another? In the next chapter, we look at how the tradition of kinetic materialism has understood the significance of *relationality*.

Notes

1 See the introduction and conclusion of Paul Sinker, *Introduction to Lucretius* (Cambridge: Cambridge University Press, 1967).

2 This is not the place for a complete literature review of the myriad ways in which Lucretius has been interpreted in Western history. My point here is that very few have read him in the exact way Marx and Woolf did in terms of 'process relational indeterminacy', as defined in this book. But I encourage readers to look at Catherine Wilson, *Epicureanism at the Origins of Modernity* (Oxford: Oxford University Press, 2008); David Norbrook, Stephen Harrison and Philip Hardie, *Lucretius and the Early Modern* (Oxford: Oxford University Press, 2015); W. R. Johnson, *Lucretius and the Modern World* (London: Bloomsbury, 2000); Steven Greenblatt, *The Swerve: How the World Became Modern* (New York: W. W. Norton, 2011); and Pierre Vesperini, *Lucrèce: Archeologie d'un classique européen* (Paris: Fayard, 2017) to see how Lucretius' ideas have been historically interpreted. Walt Whitman, for instance, was clearly influenced in many important ways by Lucretius, but as far as I know, Whitman never mentions the swerve. Furthermore, how many people have rejected the existence of discrete atoms in Lucretius but also affirmed the fully indeterminate nature of matter, along with the non-causal, non-vital immanence of the swerve? It is a much rarer position than I first thought.

3 Karl Marx and Frederick Engels, *Marx & Engels Collected Works, Volume 1: Karl Marx 1835–43* (London: Lawrence and Wishart, 1975), 48. Hereafter *MECW*.

4 Ibid., 50.

5 I have written a history of the philosophy of motion to show how rare it is for any thinker to affirm the self-cause of motion without

any higher explanation. See Thomas Nail, *Being and Motion* (Oxford: Oxford University Press, 2019).

6 Marx and Engels, *MECW, Volume 1*, 474.

7 Ibid., 48.

8 Ibid., 441.

9 See Thomas Nail, *Lucretius I: An Ontology of Motion* (Edinburgh: Edinburgh University Press, 2018), 36.

10 Karl Marx and Frederick Engels, *Marx-Engels-Gesamtausgabe, Erste Abteilung 1: Werke, Artikel, Entwürfe* (Berlin: Dietz, 1975), 35.

11 Karl Marx, *The First Writings of Karl Marx*, trans. Paul M. Schafer (New York: Ig, 2006), 132.

12 Karl Marx and Friedrich Engels, *Capital* (Chicago: Encyclopedia Britannica, 1990), 125.

13 Marx and Engels, *MECW, Volume 1*, 50.

14 See Thomas Nail, *Marx in Motion: A New Materialist Marxism* (New York: Oxford University Press, 2020).

15 Marx and Engels, *Capital*, 711.

16 Karl Marx, *Early Writings* (London: Penguin, 2005), 361.

17 Ibid., 352.

18 For more on this, see Thomas Nail, 'Kinetic Communism', in *Marx in Motion*, 198–214.

19 For much more extended arguments, see Nail, *Marx in Motion*.

20 See Thomas Nail, *Virginia Woolf: Moments of Becoming* (Redwood City, CA: Stanford University Press, under review).

21 Virginia Woolf, *The Essays of Virginia Woolf: Volume 4: 1925–1928*, ed. Andrew McNeillie (Orlando, FL: Harcourt, 1994), 160.

22 Ibid., 161.

23 Virginia Woolf, *Moments of Being: Unpublished Autobiographical Writings*, ed. Jeanne Schulkind (New York: Harcourt Brace Jovanovich, 1976), 72.

24 Virginia Woolf, *Mrs. Dalloway* (1925) (Orlando, FL: Harvest/Harcourt, 1981), 8.

25 Woolf, *Moments of Being*, 72.

26 Ibid.

27 Woolf, *Mrs. Dalloway*, 8.

28 Ibid., 9.

29 Ibid., 152–3.

30 Ibid., 8.

31 Virginia Woolf, *Orlando: A Biography* (1928) (Orlando, FL: Harvest/Harcourt, 1956), 323.

32 Virginia Woolf, *Between the Acts* (New York: Harcourt, Brace, 1941), 215.

33 Virginia Woolf, *The Waves* (1931) (Orlando, FL: Harvest/Harcourt, 1959), 118.

34 Moments of being and certain altered states of consciousness do tend to make people less afraid of death, more open to new experiences, and sensitive to others' feelings. See Hannes Kettner, Sam Gandy, Eline C. H. M. Haijen and Robin L. Carhart-Harris, 'From Egoism to Ecoism: Psychedelics Increase Nature Relatedness in a State-Mediated and Context-Dependent Manner', *Int. J. Environ. Res. Public Health* 16, no. 24 (2019): 5147. See also Paul K. Piff, Pia Dietze, Matthew Feinberg, Daniel M. Stancato and Dacher Keltner, 'Awe, the Small Self, and Prosocial Behavior', *Journal of Personality and Social Psychology* 108, no. 6 (2015): 883–99.

35 For a more fully developed account, see Nail, 'Moments of Being Political', in *Virginia Woolf: Moments of Becoming.*

36 See Carlo Rovelli, '"Incerto tempore, incertisque loci": Can We Compute the Exact Time at which a Quantum Measurement Happens?', *Foundation of Physics* 28 (1998): 1031–43. I do not agree with Rovelli's idea of randomness; see Thomas Nail, *Theory of the Object* (Edinburgh: Edinburgh University Press, 2021).

37 Sean Carroll, 'The First Quantum Cosmologist', *Discover Magazine*, 21 August 2008, https://www.discovermagazine.com/the-sciences/the-first-quantum-cosmologist (accessed 28 April 2023).

38 Ramón Román-Alcalá, 'Deviations and Uncertainty: The Concept of Swerve in Epicurus and Lucretius and Quantum Mechanics', in *4th International Multidisciplinary Scientific Conference on Social Sciences and Arts*, Vienna, 28–31 March 2017, Vol. 17, Book 2, 225–36, DOI: 10.5593/SGEMSOCIAL2017/HB21/S06.028.

39 Brian Dodson, 'Modern Truths Found in Ancient Philosophies', *Scientia, American Association for the Advancement of Science*, 6 October 2011, https://www.aaas.org/modern-truths-found-ancient-philosophies (accessed 28 April 2023).

40 'The swerve has more recently been put forward as the precursor to Heisenberg's uncertainty principle and an image for the spark that lit the Renaissance's blue touch paper.' Emma Woolerton, 'Lucretius, part 3: Chaos and Order', *The Guardian*, 4 February 2013, https://www.theguardian.com/commentisfree/2013/feb/04/lucretius-part-3-chaos-order (accessed 28 April 2023). See also Mark Kirby-Hirst, 'Epicurus on Swerving Atoms: A Modern Scientific Appraisal', *Phronimon* 10, no. 1 (2009): 43–55.

41 David Sedley, 'Lucretius', in *The Stanford Encyclopedia of Philosophy*, ed. Edward N. Zalta, https://plato.stanford.edu/archives/win2018/entries/lucretius (accessed 28 April 2023).

42 For a global hidden variables perspective, see Sean Carroll, *Something Deeply Hidden: Quantum Worlds and the Emergence of Spacetime* (Boston: Dutton, 2019). Other physicists choose instead to treat the issue of indeterminacy probabilistically. See Arthur Fine, 'Do Correlations Need to be Explained?', in James Cushing and Ernan McMullin (eds), *Philosophical Consequences of Quantum Theory* (Notre Dame, IN: University of Notre Dame Press, 1989), 175–94. They cannot know what nature will do, but they can make excellent guesses based on previous behaviour. This way, they do not have to worry about the nature of indeterminacy; they can just try to manage it.

43 For a wonderful and highly synthetic account and critique of most major interpretations of quantum mechanics, see Carlo Rovelli, *Helgoland: Making Sense of the Quantum Revolution* (New York: Riverhead Books, 2021), ch. 2.

44 See Nail, *Theory of the Object*.

45 Sean Carroll, 'A World of Vibrations', in *Something Deeply Hidden: Quantum Worlds and the Emergence of Spacetime* (London: OneWorld, 2021), 247–66. See also Karen Barad, 'Transmaterialities: Trans*/matter/realities and Queer Political Imaginings', *GLQ: A Journal of Lesbian and Gay Studies* 21 (2015): 387–422.

46 Barad, 'Transmaterialities', 396.

47 Ibid., 393. Barad's comparison is to a certain reading of the Hebrew Bible which refers to older pre-Semitic and Babylonian myths of generative void. See Nail, *Being and Motion*, 224–35.

48 A.B., 'Using Maths to Explain the Universe', *The Economist*, 2 July 2013, https://www.economist.com/prospero/2013/07/02/using-maths-to-explain-the-universe (accessed 28 April 2023).

49 John Polkinghorne, *Quantum Theory: A Very Short Introduction* (Oxford: Oxford University Press, 2002), 74.

50 Frank Close, *The Infinity Puzzle: Quantum Field Theory and the Hunt for an Orderly Universe* (New York: Basic Books, 2011), 5.

51 Ibid., 42.

52 Stephen Battersby, 'It's Confirmed: Matter is Merely Vacuum Fluctuations', *New Scientist*, 20 November 2008, https://www.newscientist.com/article/dn16095-its-confirmed-matter-is-merely-vacuum-fluctuations/ (accessed 28 April 2023).

53 While there is still no consensus in physics on how best to interpret quantum vacuum fluctuations, no one denies the *experimental* fact that there are modulations of energy below the level of empirical observation and determinate particles.

II. Relationality

Chapter 3

Ancient Relationality:
Minoan Epiphany, Archaic Oracles
and Lucretius' Muses

What is a relation? We tend to think of relations as things that connect other things. We say that point A is *related to* point B in time, in space, or causally. We say that point A is five minutes away from point B or one mile away from point B, or that when point A hits point B, it will cause it to move on to point C. This definition of a relation treats matter as a discrete, self-identical substance at a particular position. If one follows this definition, one understands motion as a change in position within a homogeneous spacetime of possible locations. This way of thinking follows the 'extensive' description of matter and motion that I presented in Chapter 1.

However, if matter and motion are *indeterminate*, as I proposed in Chapters 1 and 2, this extensive definition of relations does not work. If relations are not determinate things, what are they? This chapter and the next answer this question from within the ancient and modern tradition of kinetic materialism.

What is Relationality?

For a kinetic materialist, an 'indeterminate relation' is a process, not a discrete thing that connects other things. Relations do not designate a matrix of possible positions

in a static or even relativistic space and time. Nor is relation reducible to causality. An indeterminate relationship is
a degree of *simultaneous reciprocal change* in an open process.

In other words, there are not first isolated and enclosed
objects that enter into a relationship. Nor are there first relationships that crystallise into objects. From an indeterminate
perspective, there is no such thing as 'a relation' because
relationships are not discrete things. Furthermore, there is
no ontological difference between *relations* and that-which-
they-relate, or their *relata*. Relations and *relata* are only var-
ying degrees of reciprocal simultaneous change. They are
like waves in water.

For instance, when we look around us, we can watch
things move from point A to point B: a tree branch sways
in the wind. But this is only the tip of the iceberg. We do
not see the swarm of indeterminate processes that make up
the branch and the wind. There are no discrete identical
points in these processes, no essences, no isolated objects,
and no static background space filled with successive discrete moments in time.

When we see a branch sway in the air from one point
to another, the whole world changes. The world transforms
such that each metastable region simultaneously redistrib-
utes itself relative to the others. This global change only
seems discrete relative to our local perspective. Point A is
not a *relata*, and line AB is not a *relation*. The whole structure
is relationally constituted and relationally changed together
all at once.

Imagine, for instance, objects radiating heat as they move
from one place to another. As they move, they change.
Imagine further that as things move along their path, the
movement of everything around them changes, like a fish
in water. This alteration is what happens as the radiation

of heat affects everything around it. Even space and time are warped ever so slightly by the gravity of the object as it moves. We just don't see these things.

Think of the way a river moves. As it flows, it changes the whole of what it is through evaporation, erosion and deposition. The whole river continually changes all at once. We cannot step into the same river twice because there is no same river, us, or world. Matter and motion are not reducible to *relata* and relations because *relata* and relations are not determinate, discrete or static things. *Everything* changes with *every* change.

It is all a matter of degree. Objects change as they move, but typically they change just a little at a time. From a coarse-grain human-scale view, we could say that we roll 'a ball' from 'one side' of 'a table' to the 'other side' of the 'same' table – even though the ball, table and our bodies are all continually changing at a material level in the process of rolling. The changing relations of ball and table are reciprocal but do not change one another in equal ways. If matter and motion are indeterminate, then no two processes can be strictly equal or identical to themselves, much less to one another. In other words, changing relations are not changing relations *of* an unchanging substance or complete set of relations.

Each changed relationship is a change in the whole because the whole is relationally indeterminate. This is not the same as saying that there is a 'flat ontology' where all beings are equal. In the philosophical view I am tracing in this book, objects are metastable processes that continually change along with everything else. They do so in *asymmetrical* ways with different degrees of entanglement. There is no equality or flatness among things whatsoever.

For example, the size of an object is relative to the shape of space and time at that point. Where spacetime contracts, the object will be relatively smaller than another in a less contracted region. There is no standard, static spacetime to compare relational changes. This asymmetry is the lesson of general relativity. Furthermore, the larger the spacetime region, the more relationally entangled it is with its area. The more a part is entangled, the more energy it will dissipate through entropy. If I mix some cream into my coffee, I am increasing the entanglement and entropy of the coffee such that I cannot reverse the process of the dissipation of cream. In other words, relationality is fundamentally asymmetrical, irreversible and continually changing.

Globally, everything is related to everything else in the universe to some degree, no matter how trivial. I will discuss this more in the section on quantum physics in Chapter 4. This entanglement means that there is nothing in the universe that is wholly discrete or isolated. For this reason, there are no independent observers. Every observer (including non-human observers) affects what they are observing. Nothing is radically free to move in any way it wants, untethered from relations to something else. There is no utterly random motion either. Nor is anything entirely determined by anything external to the universe, since there is nothing outside the world. The distribution of spacetime and the degrees of entanglement that we see in our universe are emergent features, not a priori laws.

Ever since the Big Bang, the universe has been weaving and unweaving all its relational differences. It continues to experiment. Each singular distinction unfolds out of and depends on others.

If matter and motion are indeterminate, it also means that there is nothing we can call a discrete 'whole' universe. Each change in the cosmos is not a change in a background set of possible relations but a real change of the cosmos itself, such that we are no longer dealing with the same universe. All of nature observes itself, and each observation changes the relationship of nature to itself. This continual change is why relationality and indeterminacy entail one another.

Indeterminate material processes are tessellated, nested and iterated within one another. Each relational change responds to the others without fully determining the others and without being radically free from them either. Trees branch out in response to numerous changing conditions (heat, light, wind, season and other branches) but not randomly or deterministically.

In short, the 'relations' in relational materialism are global changes in the open and indeterminate process of nature. Nature is not the same nature after each change, nor is it entirely different. It is neither discontinuous nor continuous with itself. Nature has no identity because it is an indeterminate process. Relationality, therefore, is an ongoing, irreversible and asymmetrical change of matter and motion.

Let us try to trace the genealogy of this idea in the history of kinetic materialism.

Ancient Relationality

The Minoans and Archaic Greeks did not believe in independent observers or objective knowledge. For them, the knower was always inside the world where knowing occurred.[1] This has a number of consequences for how we know the world.

Minoan Epiphany

Most scholars describe Minoan religion as 'epiphanic'.[2] That is, when the Minoans wanted to know something, they

73

created a particular relationship to a place, at a specific time, in a specific bodily and mental state.[3] In this performance of knowing, a 'vision' would come to them and change them in some way. This was a highly *relational* way of knowing that assumed that what is known was also fundamentally relational to the knower.

The word 'epiphany' comes from the Greek word *epiphaneia*, meaning 'an appearing'. *Epiphaneia* is a 'vision' in the broadest sense of the term. It shows or uncovers knowledge through sensuous experiences of sight, smell, sound, thought, touch, taste and dreams. We can relate epiphany to what the Greeks later called *gnosis*, or 'knowledge through direct awareness, perception, familiarity, or observation'. Gnostic knowledge was in contrast to what the Greeks called *episteme*, from the Greek root *hístēmi*, meaning 'to stop', 'stand still', 'stay' or 'stand up'. *Gnosis* was knowledge *through* action, process and movement, but *episteme* was knowledge *of* static, frozen or rigid forms.

Since the earliest archaeological excavations of Crete, all the evidence has suggested that epiphany was central to Minoan religion.[4] Minoan religious art depicts ritual events where people gathered and raised their arms in the air and saw visions of floating plants, animals, insects and humanoid figures. Raised arms are a well-known gesture of epiphany in other cultures as well.[5] We can relate this experience of revelatory visions to what the Greeks would later call *ékstasis*, from *exístēmi*, meaning 'to change position, excite, or move away from a static position'. In the act of *ékstasis*, one began to move away from the frozen forms of epistemic knowledge towards a more performative and relational way of knowing.

Minoan art also depicted epiphany events where a female figure, typically seated under or near a tree, hands out poppy

Figure 3.1 Gold ring from Vapheio, CMS I.219. Corpus der minoischen und mykenischen Siegel.

Figure 3.2 Gold ring from Sellopoulo, HM 1034.

pods and enacts a vision for a group of others. That Minoan epiphany was always depicted in natural landscapes also strongly suggests that the landscape played a relational role in the experience of knowledge. According to the archaeologist Caroline Tully, Minoan images of epiphany express

Figure 3.3 Gold ring from Isopata, Crete, CMS II.3 No. 51. Corpus der minoischen und mykenischen Siegel.

Figure 3.4 Gold ring from Mycenae CMS I.17. Corpus der minoischen und mykenischen Siegel.

'a communicative *relationship* between a human figure and the animate landscape', such that the 'distinction [between human and nature] seems to be deliberately blurred'.[6]

Other scholars have similarly concluded that Minoan epiphanic knowledge involved a deeply relational feeling of *interconnection* with the world.[7] If this is true, it suggests that the Minoans recognised at least this one relational way of knowing. Based on the images reproduced here, Minoan ecstasy appears to involve trees, rocks, animals, insects, stars and humans, all moving and changing together as an interrelated process.

Archaeologists discovered a beautiful gold ring in a tomb at Isopata near the Minoan city of Knossos that features one of the most famous Minoan epiphany images (figure 3.3). Snakes, insects, birds and human figures all float together in front of several ecstatic dancers. In the moment of vision, mineral, animal, vegetable, human and celestial bodies mix in a shape-shifting process. The ring image shows that the theme of ambiguity 'between determinate states' is also a *relational* one of interconnection between different moving bodies.

The practice of using psychoactive drugs also speaks to the centrality of relationality in Minoan epiphany. Archaeologically, it is well established that the ancient Minoans processed opium poppies and used them in their rituals.[8] Scholars have also speculated that the Minoans used the hallucinogenic mandrake fruit that grew wild on Crete.[9] Minoan artefacts depict ecstatic rituals with poppy pods and people shaking a fruit-laden plant with extreme animation (see figure 3.1).

Why is this important philosophically? Psychotropic drug use is evidence that, for the Minoans, knowledge was a materially transformative event that one underwent with the surrounding ecology. Plant knowledge is relational knowledge that one gains by mixing the plant and its ecology directly with one's body and mind.[10] In this way, the mind and body become part plant, and the plant becomes part human. This epiphanic method of knowing is philosophically consistent with a belief in relational indeterminacy, but of course, there are other consistent methods as well.

Minoan ritual drug use may also have been a precursor to the later Greek understanding of *pharmakon*. For the Greeks, a *pharmakon* encompassed a wide range of different interwoven phenomena such as poisons, drugs, medicines, sorcery, religion, rhetoric and philosophy.[11]

Furthermore, the Minoan depiction of epiphanic events in specific places and with particular *postures* suggests a highly relational performance. Since the world was relational for the Minoans, they could not attain knowledge equally anywhere or anytime. Ecstatic knowledge occurred not in but *through* singular places, trees, rocks and animals. To know the world, the Minoans went down into earthen caves.[12] They climbed up to mountain shrines. They sat under trees and laid their bodies on boulders. To know was to be in a transformative relationship to a place. These Minoan rituals also influenced how the Archaic Greeks thought about religion and knowledge.[13]

Archaic Oracles

For the Archaic Greeks, oracular knowledge was a relational way of knowing something. Oracular truths were not statements of universal fact that could be understood equally by anyone, anywhere, anytime. Instead, an oracular revelation was an experience or state of mind that happened *to* or *through* the knower. The Archaic Greeks had a beautiful word for this, *aletheia*, which means 'truth through revelation'. It was a wonderfully 'ambiguous' and relational understanding of truth, as Marcel Detienne has argued.[14] Like the Minoans, the Archaic Greeks believed that knowing or *aletheia* was something that one *underwent* in a specific place, time or aesthetic performance.

This was the kind of knowledge at work in the most important oracle of the Greek world: the oracle of Delphi. For thousands of years, the oracle of Delphi was considered the most sacred source of knowledge in the Greek world. But before its occupation by Apollo, the god of prophecy, it was a pre-Archaic spring. According to the 'Hymn to Apollo', written around the sixth century BCE, before Apollo arrived, a water nymph named Telphusa listened carefully to a freshwater spring in an 'undisturbed forest clearing' (*choros apēmōn*) and interpreted its oracular babbling for those who sought wisdom.[15] At least one archaeologist has discovered the remains of a pre-Greek shrine near Delphi that he believes was Telphusa's oracle.[16]

In his hymn, Homer says that Hera gave birth to a female dragon named Delphyne to guard Telphusa's oracle. That it was Hera and a serpent that protected the oracle is a strong indication that the Greeks originally connected Telphusa's spring with the pre-Greek Minoan snake-priestess and her sacred woodland or *chora*.[17] The serpent's spiralled shape also echoes the spiral meander patterns indicative of ambiguity in the Minoan worldview.[18]

Later in the hymn, Apollo is searching for an oracle where he can build his own sacred 'dendritic grove' (*alsea dendrenta*) when he comes upon Delphyne and suspects that she may be guarding an oracle. He kills the dragon and covers her body with a mountain.[19]

Thus spoke the lord, far-working Apollo, and pushed over upon her a crag with a shower of rocks, hiding her streams: and he made himself an altar in a wooded grove very near the clear-flowing stream. In that place, all men pray to the great one by the name Telphusian, because he humbled the stream of holy Telphusa.[20]

Not only did Apollo bury the clear flowing streams with a mountain, he also buried the rotting body of the dragon that the poet of the hymn then calls 'Python', from the Greek word *púthein*, 'to rot'. This is why Apollo is called 'Pythian Apollo' and 'Telphusian Apollo', and the oracle is called the Delphic oracle, after Delphyne.

After this event, the hymn tells us that Apollo appointed women from the Cretan city of Knossos to be the oracular priestesses or Delphic 'bees'. This is another textual indication that the Archaic Greeks believed that the tradition of oracular knowledge originally came from the Minoans and their snake and bee priestesses. The Cretan priestesses sat on a tripod inside the mountain positioned over the chasm left by Python, and supposedly inhaled the fumes emanating from Python's rotting body deep in Mother Earth. Whether it was fumes from incense or volcanic gases or neither is debated.[21] But whatever happened induced an altered state of consciousness, causing the priestesses to channel the sacred words of Earth into oracular truth.

In addition to these fumes, the Pythian priestesses would also drink a bowl of spring water mixed with the wild herbs or 'laurels' that grew around the oracle. Some scholars have argued that these herbal potions may have also induced altered states of consciousness that facilitated oracular speech.[22] Outside the mountain cave at Delphi there was also an enormous boulder that was said to be the one that Cronos spat up instead of baby Zeus. The Greeks believed this boulder was an *omphalos* or navel of the Earth, which scholars have also compared to the *baetyl* rocks hugged by worshippers during Minoan rituals.[23]

But what philosophical conclusions can we draw from the oracular nature of truth at Delphi? For the Archaic Greeks, oracular knowledge occurred in a sacred place at certain seasons through a careful physiological interpretation of water's sounds and the ingestion of psychoactive fumes and plants. The Cretan priestesses at Delphi were not ultra-rational geniuses who could see the objective future with universal foresight. They were not isolated contemplators of abstract unchanging truth. Instead, they were vessels through which the words of a dying snake moved materially and relationally.

This is one important and relational way that certain Archaic Greeks knew the world, namely allowing matter to flow into their bodies and transform them. They did not think of humans or human knowledge as separate from nature. If they did, how would nature move through them? Since the Greeks believed that seasonal psychoactive vapours and/or herbs transmitted knowledge, this strongly suggests that they believed in at least one relational and performative kind of knowledge shared by the Minoans.

They believed that the gods were aspects or dimensions of processual reality. The gods were shape-changers who spoke out of the Earth and through plants.[24] The Greeks may have believed their gods were undying, but, at least according to Homer, that did not mean they were not relationally affected by the world.[25]

Lucretius in the Mountains of the Muses

This Archaic oracular understanding of truth also influenced Lucretius, who developed it into his own relational materialism. One of the most explicit and deeply anti-Epicurean examples of oracular relationality in Lucretius' poem is when he says that the source of his knowledge of the obscure nature of things comes from being stabbed in the heart by Dionysus' spear or 'thyrsus'.[26] After Dionysus stabs him, Lucretius says that his intoxicated mind 'blooms' and opens up like a flower. Like one of Dionysus' satyrs, Lucretius then says he wanders through the mountains of the Muses, drinking from hidden springs.

> I am very aware how obscure [the nature of things] are.
> But great hope for praise strikes my heart with a sharp
>   thyrsus
> and at the same time strikes into my breast sweet love
> for the Muses. Now roused by this in my flourishing
>   mind
> I am traversing the remote places of the Pierides,
>   untrodden by the
> sole of anyone before.[27]

The great hope of knowing the indeterminate nature of things penetrates Lucretius' heart (for him, the seat of the mind) and strikes him like a sharp thyrsus. The thyrsus is a symbol of fertility, pleasure and intoxication. The wand was made of fennel and had a pine cone full of seeds on the end of it. In ancient Greece, Dionysian celebrants dipped their thyrsus *spears* in honey. This connected the spear to the tradition of the oracular bees and the psychoactive mead made from mountain herbs and wild honey, which they also stirred with the thyrsus.[28]

In other words, Lucretius described an altered state of consciousness connected with the oracular tradition of Delphi, where worshippers celebrated Dionysus in the winter.[29] Through the introduction of matter into his body in the form of mind-altering substances, Lucretius' 'mind blooms' (*mente vigenti*)[30] like the tree god himself, Dendrites Dionysus. In this way, Lucretius says he comes to know the world, not through quiet contemplation, but through the material transformation of his body and mind into the branching world. This poetic image directly connects his concepts of matter as forest, tree and sprout (*materies, corpora, semina*) to his oracular method of knowing matter.

Lucretius then says he wanders the remote, obscure, wild, mountainous regions of the Muses in this intoxicated state, where no one has gone before. In the mountains, Lucretius drinks from the mysterious 'flowing source' of all things (*fontes*).

It is a joy to approach pure springs
and to drink from them, and it is a joy to pick new
    flowers
and to seek a pre-eminent crown for my head from that
    place
whence the Muses had wreathed the temples of no one
    before.[31]

Lucretius receives 'pleasure' from the 'undivided' and hidden flows of water, just like those who drank from Telphusa's forest spring and Delphi's mountain spring.

Lucretius picks the young mountain flowers and forms them into a laurel wreath around his head, just as Bacchus did at Delphi. But the laurels at Delphi may have also been oleander laurels, which were oracular intoxicants that made the mind come alive like a plant.[32] In this way, Lucretius says he frees his mind not by removing an external obstacle but by transforming his inner material bodily state.

But by far the most dramatic scene of relational knowledge in Lucretius' poem happens in Book III. Immediately after reading through the 'leaves' of Epicurus' books as a 'jumping bee sips and spills pollen haphazardly in a flower-strewn meadow', Lucretius says he enters into an intoxicated state of rapture. He begins to shake and convulse with a vision of unlimited nature spread out in all directions.

> Then, from these things a kind of divine desire
> and shivering awe seizes me, because in this way nature
> by your power has been uncovered and laid open in all
> directions.[33]

Instead of a merely mental contemplation of nature, Lucretius says he experienced the 'disclosure' (*retecta*) of a vision reminiscent of the method of Archaic Greek *aletheia*. Just as matter continually swerves, according to Lucretius, so he knows it by performing the shaking rapture with his body. This is an explicitly relational way of knowing.

Elsewhere in his poem Lucretius also rejects the anti-relational view that something could come from nothing. If things could come from nothing then anything could come from anything else, he says. All fruits could grow from all trees and men could sprout from the sea.

> For if things came to be from nothing, every kind of
> thing
> could be born from all things, and nothing would need a
> sprout.[34]

But this is not what we see. Instead, we see emergent patterns increasing and changing 'little by little' in rhythms, like the seasons that repeat but slightly differently each time. The patterns are neither random nor entirely determined. Here, Lucretius beautifully contrasts the non-relational idea of *ex nihilo* creation with the Archaic relational image of branching, swerving and material sprouting. Each beansprout will grow into a bean and each plant will branch out slightly differently each time. This is because all of nature changes constantly with each change and in relationally iterative patterns.

But how did this idea of indeterminate relationality reach modern thinkers? In the next chapter, we see how Marx, Woolf and several quantum physicists picked up this ancient idea from Lucretius and carried it forward in their own ways.

Notes

1 Marcel Detienne has done interesting work especially on the Archaic concept of *aletheia* as a kind of relational practice of truth. 'Alētheia pronounces a performative truth. She is the power of efficacy and creates being.' Marcel Detienne, *The Masters of Truth in Archaic Greece*, trans. Janet Lloyd (New York: Zone Books, 1996), 16.

2 For introductions and literature reviews of Minoan epiphany, see Alan Peatfield and Christine Morris, 'Dynamic Spirituality on Minoan Peak Sanctuaries', in Kathryn Rountree, Christine Morris and Alan Peatfield (eds), *Archaeology of Spiritualities* (New York: Springer, 2012), 227–45; and Caroline Tully, 'Virtual Reality: Tree Cult and Epiphanic Ritual in Aegean Glyptic Iconography', *Journal of Prehistoric Religion* 25 (2016): 19–30.

3 Just because the Minoans did not have a concept of nature does not mean that they did not have a philosophical understanding of nature. For a similar argument with respect to the emergence of science before the concept of nature, see Francesca Rochberg, *Before Nature: Cuneiform Knowledge and the History of Science* (Chicago: University of Chicago Press, 2020). If matter and motion are indeterminate and relational then there can be no such thing as a 'trans-historical' or 'mono-naturalism' that remains the same through time. It also means that there is no 'multi-naturalism' either, since nature is continually shape-changing, indeterminate and relational. See also Brooke Holmes, 'Situating Scamander: "Natureculture" in the *Iliad*', *Ramus* 44, no. 1–2 (2015): 29–51.

I am sympathetic to the views of the Brazilian anthropologist Eduardo Viveiros de Castro and the French anthropologist Philippe Descola, who argue against the Eurocentric notion of a transhistorical 'mono-naturalism'. Such a view assumes a division between nature and culture. It also assumes that nature is all one type of passive physical stuff, while human culture is composed of plural, active mental ways of thinking. See Eduardo Viveiros de Castro, 'Perspectival Anthropology and the Method of Controlled Equivocation', *Tipití: Journal of the Society for the Anthropology of Lowland South America* 2, no. 1 (2004); and Philippe Descola, *Beyond Nature and Culture*, trans. Janet Lloyd (Chicago: University of Chicago Press, 2013). See also Eduardo Kohn, *How Forests Think: Toward an Anthropology Beyond the Human* (Berkeley: University of California Press, 2015).

However, I also find the division between 'external', 'internal', 'mono' and 'multi' categories endorsed by these thinkers to be inadequate for understanding a more indeterminate, relational and process philosophy of nature, matter and motion. Instead of contrasting 'multiculturalism' and 'multinaturalism', I am arguing instead for the existence of an historical 'indeterminate natureculturalism'. For a similar difference with the work of Eduardo Kohn, see Thomas Nail, *Theory of the Earth* (Stanford, CA: Stanford University Press, 2021), ch. 4.

4 For a full literature review of the scholarly reception of Minoan epiphany, see Tully, 'Virtual Reality', 21.

5 See ibid., for discussion.

6 Ibid., 23 (my italics), 22.

7 These images may also depict states of feeling. See Erin McGowan, 'Experiencing and Experimenting with Embodied Archaeology: Re-Embodying the Sacred Gestures of Neopalatial Minoan Crete', *Archaeological Review from Cambridge* 21, no. 2 (2006): 32–57.

8 For a full literature review of Minoan poppy usage, see Caroline Tully and Sam Crooks, 'Dropping Ecstasy? Minoan Cult and the Tropes of Shamanism', *Time and Mind: The Journal of Archaeology, Consciousness and Culture* 8, no. 2 (2015): 129–58 (137). See also Robert S. Merrillees, 'Opium for the Masses: How the Ancients Got High', *Odyssey* 2, no. 1 (1999): 29.

9 '[Dr Sabine] Beckman has suggested that mandrake may be one of the best candidates for a Minoan hallucinogen (unpublished presentation given at the 9th International Congress of Ethnobiology in Canterbury, 2004).' Tully and Crooks, 'Dropping Ecstasy?', 153.

10 For an interesting interpretation of the meaning of this plant knowledge/ communication, see Richard M. Doyle, *Darwin's Pharmacy: Sex, Plants, and the Evolution of the Noösphere* (Seattle: University of Washington Press, 2011). For interpretations of some specific Minoan ecstatic rituals, see Arthur J. Evans, *The Palace of Minos. A Comparative Account of the Successive Stages of early Cretan Civilization as illustrated by the Discoveries at*

Knossos. Vol. III (London: Macmillan, 1930), 68, 142; Arthur J. Evans, *The Palace of Minos. A Comparative Account of the Successive Stages of early Cretan Civilization as illustrated by the Discoveries at Knossos. Vol. IV* (London: Macmillan, 1936), 392. For more on the broader Indo-European origins of plant knowledge, see Gordon Wasson, *Soma: Divine Mushroom of Immortality* (New York: Harcourt Brace Jovanovich, 1967).

11 'A pharmakon could be a remedy used in medicine or an ointment applied as part of bodily training, but it could also be the basis of a spell, charm, or talisman used in sorcery or divination, and it could be an analogue to the power of the spoken word and its ability to place an audience under the influence of the speaker. What is more, in the ancient worldview understanding of these activities was deeply interwoven.' See Michael A. Rinella, *Pharmakon: Plato, Drug Culture, and Identity in Ancient Athens* (Lanham, MD: Lexington Books, 2010), xxii. See Part III of the book for a survey of the broad range of meanings of *pharmakon*. For its unique role in Plato's work, see also Jacques Derrida, 'Plato's Pharmacy', in *Dissemination*, trans. Barbara Johnson (Chicago: University of Chicago Press, 1981).

12 Loeta Tyree, 'Diachronic Changes in Minoan Cave Cult', in Robert Laffineur and Robin Hägg (eds), *POTNIA: Deities and Religion in the Aegean Bronze Age* (Liège and Austin, TX: Université de Liège and the University of Texas at Austin, 2001), 39–50.

13 One way in which the Greeks continued this tradition was through incubation rituals. For a fascinating discussion, see Hedvig von Ehrenheim, 'Greek Incubation Rituals in Classical and Hellenistic Times', PhD dissertation, Stockholm University, 2011, 39–50.

14 For a treatment of this idea and its difference from classical Greek knowledge, see Detienne, *The Masters of Truth*.

15 Homer, 'Hymn to Apollo', line 244. My translation.

16 Joseph Fontenrose, 'The Spring Telphusa', *Transactions and Proceedings of the American Philological Association* 100 (1969): 119–31.

17 For the connection between Hera and Minoan Crete, see Carl Kerenyi, *Dionysos: Archetypal Image of Indestructible Life*, trans. Ralph Manheim (Princeton, NJ: Princeton University Press, 1976), 116. See also Thomas Nail, *Being and Motion* (Oxford: Oxford University Press, 2019), ch. 19.

18 Robert B. Koehl, 'The Ambiguity of the Minoan Mind', in Eva Alram-Stern, Fritz Blakolmer, Sigrid Deger-Jalkotzy, Robert Laffineur and Jörg Weilhartner (eds), *Metaphysis: Ritual, Myth and Symbolism in the Aegean Bronze Age. 15th International Aegean Conference, University of Vienna, 22–25 April 2014* (Leuven: Peeters, 2016), 470.

19 Homer, 'Hymn to Apollo', line 245. My translation.

20 Homer, 'Hymn to Apollo', in *The Homeric Hymns*, ed. and trans. Susan Shelmerdine (Newburyport, MA: Focus Publishing, 1995), lines 375–85.

21 For a review of the literature on the geological debates about volcanic fumes, see Iain S. Stewart and Luigi Piccardi, 'Seismic Faults and Sacred Sanctuaries in Aegean Antiquity', *Proceedings of the Geologists' Association* 128 (2017): 711–21. See section 5.1 on Delphi.

22 Haralampos Harissis, 'A Bittersweet Story: The True Nature of the Laurel of the Oracle of Delphi', *Perspectives in Biology and Medicine* 57, no. 3 (2014): 351–60.

23 Nanno Marinatos, 'The Character of Minoan Epiphanies', *Illinois Classical Studies* 29 (2004): 25–42 (32). See also John Younger, 'Tree Tugging and Omphalos Hugging on Minoan Gold Rings', *Hesperia Supplements* 42 (2009): 43–9.

24 See note 3 for a discussion of Descola's views on naturalism. I am not trying to equate or differentiate all Minoan religion from all Archaic Greek religion as Descola attempts. I am only pointing out the emergence of some aspects of relationality at work in Minoan and Archaic Greek practices of truth.

25 See Lorenzo Garcia, *Homeric Durability: Telling Time in the Iliad* (Washington, DC: Center for Hellenic Studies, 2013).

26 Titus Lucretius Carus, *De Rerum Natura (On the Nature of Things)*, ed. Walter Englert (Newburyport, MA: Focus Publishing, 2003), 1.922–30.

27 Ibid., 1.921–6.

28 Gordon Wasson, Albert Hofmann and Carl A. P. Ruck, *The Road to Eleusis: Unveiling the Secret of the Mysteries* (Berkeley, CA: North Atlantic Books, 2008), 98. Ruck notes how Theophrastus records that 'herb gatherers used to stuff their cuttings into hollow, fennel-like stalks to preserve their freshness'.

29 The explicit reference to the oracle Delphi occurs at 1.734–41 in *De Rerum Natura*. See Thomas Nail, *Lucretius I: An Ontology of Motion* (Edinburgh: Edinburgh University Press, 2017), ch. 8.

30 Lucretius, *De Rerum Natura*, 1.925.

31 Ibid., 1.927–34.

32 For details of this interesting hypothesis, see Harissis, 'A Bittersweet Story'.

33 Lucretius, *De Rerum Natura*, 3.28–9.

34 Ibid., 1.156–7.

Chapter 4

Modern Relationality: Marx's Metabolism, Woolf's Rapture and Quantum Entanglement

Marx's Metabolism

Marx did not adopt the ancient practice of oracular truth and ecstasy. Still, he took from Lucretius the more general idea of 'sensuous' relational practice as the basis of knowledge and politics. In his dissertation, Marx argued that all of nature had sensation in a broad sense, not just humans. Humans, for Marx, are only a particular expression of a broader 'sensuous world'.[1] Marx also argued that the 'practical motion', or what he later called 'theoretical practice', always begins from material sensation and not from ideal thought or contemplation.[2] According to Marx, philosophy 'proceeds from the sphere of the sensuous',[3] just as he said it did for Lucretius.

Specifically, in his dissertation, Marx got close to paraphrasing Lucretius' more poetic theory of knowledge when he described 'moments when philosophy turns its eyes to the external world, and no longer apprehends it, but, as a practical person, weaves, as it were, intrigues with the world'.[4] Lucretius frequently used this same 'weaving' image in his poetry. I am not the only one to pick up on the fact that Marx got his idea of the primacy of practice from Lucretius. The English editor of Marx's dissertation writes that 'The seeds of

[Marx's] "revolutionizing praxis" are already present in his dissertation writings.'[5]

To my mind, this is nowhere more obvious than in Marx's *Theses on Feuerbach*, which connect his dissertation writings to his later political writings. Marx writes that

> The chief defect of all previous materialism (that of Feuerbach included) is that things, reality, sensuousness are conceived only in the form of the object, or of contemplation, but not as sensuous human activity, practice, not subjectively. Hence, in contradistinction to materialism, the active side was set forth abstractly by idealism – which, of course, does not know real, sensuous activity as such.[6]

Here, Marx rejects the idealist definition of matter and motion as mental 'objects' or categories of thought. This is also why Marx rejected Democritus' atomism. For Marx, Democritus reduced the knowledge of matter to 'abstract individuals' (atoms) of ideal contemplation.[7] In this way, Marx believed that Democritus became a sceptic of the sensual world because he believed one could not *sense* the fundamental objects of matter (atoms). Here, Marx says, 'the concept of the atom and sensuous perception face each other as enemies. Thus Democritus does not escape the antinomy.'[8]

By contrast, Marx followed the relational and sensuous materialism of Lucretius. Indeed, he wrote in his *Theses on Feuerbach* that

> The question whether objective truth can be attributed to human thinking is not a question of theory but is a practical question. Man must prove the truth, i.e., the reality and power, the this-worldliness of his thinking in practice. The dispute over the reality or nonreality of thinking which is isolated from practice is a purely scholastic question.[9]

For Marx, like Lucretius, knowledge is always performative, practical and local.[10] The truth of the world emerges through relations of motion, not through contemplation or mental representation. This is why, for Marx, 'the coincidence of the changing of circumstances and of human activity or self-change can be conceived and rationally understood only as revolutionary practice'.[11] In short, Marx took Lucretius' idea of relational knowledge and emphasised its political power to transform nature and human society.

Later in his life, Marx gave this sensuous relational process another significant name: 'metabolism'. Marx's concept of metabolism is one of his most important ideas and is at the heart of his relational materialism. The German word for metabolism is *Stoffwechsel*, from the German words *Stoff*, meaning 'matter', and *Wechsel*, meaning 'change'. Metabolism, for Marx, was how the entire world of nature and human society constantly and relationally changed.

Before Marx started using the word 'metabolism', he called it 'hanging-together' (*zusammenhängenden*). 'The whole of sensuous certainty will be considered as this fluctuating process', he wrote in his dissertation.[12] In his *1844 Manuscripts*, Marx wrote that all living beings maintain themselves as constant, continual processes of relational hanging-together within the inorganic body of nature.[13] All beings flow and hang together in relations of mutual interdependence. They co-produce *one another* through inorganic material processes. 'That man's physical and spiritual life hang together with nature means simply that nature hangs together relationally with itself, for man is a part of nature.'[14]

In the widest sense, Marx called this the 'universal metabolism' or 'universal metabolic process' of 'nature's metabolism'.[15] Within nature's metabolism there is a 'metabolic interaction between man and nature'[16] or a 'human metabolism with nature'.[17] Human societies then emerge from nature as an 'interdependent process of social metabolism'.[18] Through this 'material and mental metabolism',[19] living human individuals 'change ... in that they bring out new qualities in themselves, develop themselves in production, transform themselves, develop new powers and ideas, new modes of intercourse, new needs and new language'.[20]

Marx even based his idea of communism on relational metabolism. For Marx, communism was the maintenance of a relational 'balance between expenditure and income',[21] of material production and consumption, for the proper 'restoration, renewal and refreshment'[22] of the 'powers of life',[23] the 'vitality of the soil'[24] and the 'realm of natural forces'.[25] The importance of this metabolic balance is also why, according to Marx,

> Communism, as fully developed naturalism, equals humanism, and as fully developed humanism equals naturalism; it is the genuine resolution of the conflict between man and nature and between man and man – the true resolution of the strife between existence and essence, between objectification and self-confirmation, between freedom and necessity, between the individual and the species.[26]

Ontological and ecological relationality was, therefore, at the heart of Marx's philosophical and political project. Metabolism was not discrete relations between discrete *relata*. It was the 'hanging-together' of nature as an open and simultaneously changing process. For Marx, metabolism and communism are the natural, human and social balance of the global relationality that capitalism continually ignores and disrupts using hierarchy and the value-form, as I discussed in Chapter 2.[27]

Woolf's Rapture

Virginia Woolf also came to her relational materialism partly through Lucretius, although Woolf emphasised the *poetic* and *aesthetic* dimensions of relationality
more than Marx did. For instance, her interest in relational epiphany is apparent in her annotated copy of
Lucretius' *De Rerum Natura*. Woolf did not annotate
and translate the whole or even most of *De Rerum
Natura*, but instead focused primarily on very particular moments in the text. Specifically, she focused
on Lucretius' three epiphanies: 1) his divine vision
of Venus;[28] 2) his intoxicated wandering through the
mountains of the Muses;[29] and 3) his shaking rapture after seeing the unlimited universe in Epicurus'
writings.[30]

The single most frequent word translated in Woolf's
copy of *De Rerum Natura* is 'shock', which is also the word
she used to describe her own 'moments of being'. The next
most frequent word in her English translation is 'whirl',
from the Latin word *raptum*, meaning rapture.[31] Among
her very few annotations in Book III, she chose to translate
the most dramatic and explicit moment of epiphany in all
of Lucretius: *divina voluptas … atque horror* as the 'thrilling awe of rapture'.[32] Woolf then used the term 'thrilling'
to describe one of her characters' moments of ecstasy in
her novel *Mrs. Dalloway*, writing that 'The earth *thrilled*
beneath him.'[33]

In her autobiography, Woolf wrote that she experienced
moments of existential 'shock' and 'rapture' that revealed to
her the hidden relational network beneath the cotton wool
of the seemingly discrete objects of everyday life. She wrote
that these moments

will become a revelation of some order; it is a token
of some real thing behind appearances; and I make it
real by putting it into words. It is only by putting it
into words that I make it whole; ... It is the rapture
I get when in writing I seem to be discovering what
belongs to what; ... that behind the cotton wool is
hidden a pattern; that we – I mean all human beings –
are connected with this; that the whole world is a work
of art; that we are parts of the work of art. Hamlet or a
Beethoven quartet is the truth about this vast mass that
we call the world. But there is no Shakespeare, there is
no Beethoven; certainly and emphatically there is no
God; we are the words; we are the music; we are the
thing itself. And I see this when I have a shock.[34]

Beneath the world of discrete objects, Woolf saw the ordered
relations and processes that weave reality together. This reality was not an objective, observer-independent world. It
was only *through* the relational process of her own writing
practice that she 'wove' herself into this process to know it.

For Woolf, the pattern hidden behind the cotton wool
connected all human beings, words and nature. 'We are the
words; we are the thing itself.' With this simple statement,
Woolf did what few in the history of European philosophy before her had ever dared. She overturned the division
between the for-itself and the in-itself. In other words, for
Woolf, there are no relations or *relata*, but rather a continually changing natural world.

Woolf was not interested in unchanging Platonic forms.
For her, it was impossible to know forms without performatively affecting them. In this way, Woolf invented a
relational and material literary technique based on performative moments of knowing. Art and literature, for her, do
not represent the world to produce forms that are superior to the materiality of the sensuous moment. Instead, for

Woolf, the arts aim to expose the world's indeterminate relationality and weave new sensations with it.

Woolf described a fully relational world of motion: 'a world where each part depends upon the other, the serene, impersonal, and indestructible world of art'.[35] Woolf's world of art is not one of interior monologues but of impersonal processes and transformations. She said she wanted to 'achieve a symmetry by means of infinite discords, showing all the traces of the mind's passage through the world'.[36] Word and mind are not static or distinct but pass through one another and leave traces of their transformation. Instead of logical or ontological negation or contradiction, Woolf was interested in what she called 'discordant harmonies',[37] that is, relations of simultaneous but not necessarily harmonic change.

For Woolf, the world is not substances chopped up into discrete non-relational units. 'Life is not a series of gig lamps symmetrically arranged; life is a luminous halo, a semi-transparent envelope surrounding us from the beginning of consciousness to the end.'[38] Life is a luminous halo, for Woolf, precisely because 'human beings [are] not always in relation to each other but in *relation to reality*'.[39]

Woolf thus imagined her work as an ongoing discovery of relational patterns of motion. For example, in *Mrs. Dalloway*, the main character sees the world, not as discrete solid objects, but 'laid out like a mist [...] spread ever so far, her life, herself'.[40] For Woolf, knowledge of the fixed states of static objects was impossible, because as the waves collide and diffract, they change the water's entire relational surface. As Mrs Dalloway says, 'our apparitions, the part of us which appears, are so momentary compared with the other, the unseen part of us, which spreads wide'.[41] 'Beneath it is all dark, it is all spreading, it is unfathomably deep; but now and again we rise to the surface and that is what you see us by.'[42] Another character in *Mrs. Dalloway*, Septimus Smith, similarly sees a tree 'connected by millions of fibres with his own body'.[43] For him, the world spreads its fibres through our bodies because the world is relational.

Woolf was probably attracted to Lucretius' accounts of epiphany because of her own experiences. But in reading and translating his poem, she was helped in her understanding of them and their integration into a larger naturalistic philosophical framework offered by Lucretius. There were many influences on Woolf's understanding of her epiphanic moments, but Lucretius was certainly a major influence for her.[44]

Quantum Entanglement

Contemporary physicists may have left behind the ancient practice of oracle, but some still adopt the idea of radical relationality in their own way. Just as certain physicists credited Lucretius with the notion of indeterminacy, they also should have credited him with the related idea of *relational* indeterminacy. Lucretius described relationality as a process of cosmic 'weaving',[45] similar to what physicists call 'quantum entanglement'.[46]

In the words of the Austrian physicist Erwin Schrödinger, 'entanglement' is '*not … one* but rather *the* characteristic trait of quantum mechanics, the one that enforces its entire departure from classical lines of thought'.[47] Quantum entanglement means that scientists cannot describe the state of a pair or group of particles independently of others' states. Entanglement occurs even when vast distances separate the particles. Their materiality and motion are relational. The measurement of the position, momentum, spin and polarisation of one entangled particle correlates with other entangled particles. In quantum physics, it is not possible to specify a system's state by listing the state of all its subsystems or local regions *individually*. 'We have to look at the system as a whole, because different parts of it can be entangled with one another.'[48]

In 1935 Albert Einstein, Boris Podolsky and Nathan Rosen famously argued that if entanglement were true, quantum physics would be incomplete, since it could not predict each discrete change independently. If it were complete, they argued, then it would have to be *non-local* – which would imply that distant agents were acting on local ones without any physical connection. Einstein later called this effect 'spooky action at a distance' and profoundly disagreed with it. Einstein wanted things to have objective non-relational properties, whether they were measured or not. He wrote:

> That which really exists in B should not depend on what kind of measurement is carried out in part of space A; it should also be independent of whether or not any measurement at all is carried out in space A. If one adheres to this program, one can hardly consider the quantum-theoretical description as a complete representation of the physically real. If one tries to do so in spite of this, one has to assume that the physically real in B suffers a sudden change as a result of a measurement in A. My instinct for physics bristles at this.[49]

Einstein was all right with the idea that space and time were locally relative to one another. However, he was not okay with the idea that nature was globally relational such that a change in one distant location would have a correlated simultaneous change in another. The so-called 'EPR paradox', named after the authors above, remained a theoretical controversy until John Bell put forward a mathematical theorem and thought experiment that proved Einstein wrong in 1964.[50] However, it was only with Alan Aspect's 1982 EPR-based experiments in Paris (repeatedly confirmed over the past forty years)[51] that entanglement (relational correlations between distant quantum events) was proven to be undeniably real. All 'local realist' theories of causality have now been proven false.[52]

This position's philosophical consequences are radical, even though there is no universally accepted interpretation of them. We experimentally know, though, that local material motions are relationally entangled and correlated with global ones. Each local region relationally entangles in some way with the rest of the universe. This entanglement does not *necessarily* mean that there is action at a distance or retroaction in time. Nor does it *necessarily* follow a deterministic global wave function for the entire universe, as David Bohm speculated.[53] Some physicists have even argued that it may be experimentally *impossible* and practically *unnecessary* to explain entanglement by a broader causal framework precisely because of quantum physics's indeterministic nature.[54] At the moment, the indeterminism of entangled relations and their emergent patterns are experimental givens of physics. No framework has experimentally shown that entanglement derives from any deeper deterministic or non-relational principle.

But if entanglement is fundamental, it means that there are no discrete relations or *relata*. There are only global relational transformations in the whole entangled universe. Each local change co-occurs and in a precise correlation with the rest of the indeterministic universe. If entanglement is fundamental, it also means that there are no discrete causes or effects because there is nothing that is not relational.

There is only a 'qualitative transformation of the whole', as the philosopher Henri Bergson was fond of saying.[55]

If entanglement is true at the tiniest scales, it is also true at the larger ones, although entanglement's immediate effects may not be perceptible. The physicist Karen Barad has explicitly tried to bridge this divide by emphasising relationality across scales. She writes that

> bodies do not simply take their places in the world. They are not simply situated in, or located in, particular environments. Rather, 'environments' and 'bodies' are intra-actively co-constituted. Bodies ('human', 'environmental', or otherwise) are integral 'parts' of, or dynamic reconfigurings of, what is.[56]

Entanglement is also central to the quantum measurement problem. Any measurement of the universe is part of and entangled with what is measured. There is no purely neutral observer or objective measurement. In the words of the physicist Carlo Rovelli,

> The [quantum] theory does not describe things as they 'are': it describes how things 'occur', and how they 'interact with each other.' It doesn't describe where there is a particle but how the particle shows itself to others. The world of existent things is reduced to a realm of possible interactions. Reality is reduced to interaction. Reality is reduced to relation.[57]

In this chapter, I have tried to show how Marx and Woolf were influenced directly by Lucretius' theory of relationality, each in their own way. I have also argued that quantum physicists have elaborated an experimental principle of relationality that resembles that of Lucretius (as I read him) and which I think they should recognise, but which they often do not. More specifically, I have argued that

Marx used the idea of relationality as the basis of his concept of sensuous practice (and metabolism) and that Woolf used it in her relational aesthetics of rapture. Quantum physicists also use it in their experimental understanding of quantum entanglement.

But how do all these indeterminate relations build up into the stable objects we see around us? In the next chapter we look at how the tradition of kinetic materialism has answered this question with the key ideas of *process* and *pattern*.

Notes

1 Karl Marx and Frederick Engels, *Marx & Engels Collected Works, Volume 1: Karl Marx 1835–43* (London: Lawrence and Wishart, 1975), 40, 45. Hereafter *MECW*.

2 Ibid., 438.

3 Ibid., 471.

4 Ibid., 491.

5 Karl Marx, *The First Writings of Karl Marx*, trans. Paul M. Schafer (New York: Ig, 2006), 57.

6 Karl Marx and Frederick Engels, *Marx & Engels Collected Works, Volume 5: Karl Marx 1845–47* (London: Lawrence & Wishart, 1976), 3.

7 Marx and Engels, *MECW, Volume 1*, 39, 50.

8 Ibid., 39.

9 Marx and Engels, *MECW, Volume 5*, 3.

10 There is no doubt that Hegel also influenced Marx's idea that truth must be proven in historical practice.

11 Ibid., 4.

12 Marx and Engels, *MECW, Volume 1*, 458.

13 Karl Marx and Frederick Engels, *Marx-Engels-Gesamtausgabe, Vol. 2* (Berlin: Dietz, 1975), 240.

14 Karl Marx and Frederick Engels, *Marx & Engels Collected Works, Volume 3: Karl Marx: March 1843–August 1844* (London: Lawrence and Wishart, 1975), 276. My translation.

15 Karl Marx and Frederick Engels, *Marx & Engels Collected Works, Volume 30: Marx: 1861–1863* (Lawrence and Wishart, 1988), 62, 63, 78.

16 Ibid., 290.

17 Karl Marx, *Capital: A Critique of Political Economy, Vol. 3*, trans. David Fernbach (New York: Penguin, 1993), 959.

18 Ibid., 949.

19 Ibid., 161.

20 Karl Marx, *Capital: A Critique of Political Economy, Vol. 2*, trans. David Fernbach (New York: Penguin, 1992), 226.

21 Karl Marx, *Theories of Surplus-Value, Part III*, trans. Jack Cohen and S. W. Ryazanskaya (Moscow: Progress Publishers, 1971), 309.

22 Karl Marx, *Capital: A Critique of Political Economy, Vol. 1*, trans. David Fernbach and Ben Fowkes (New York: Penguin, 1990), 376.

23 Karl Marx, *Economic and Philosophic Manuscripts of 1844* (London: Lawrence and Wishart, 1982), 181.

24 Marx, *Capital Vol. 3*, 949.

25 Ibid., 964. See Paul Burkett and John Bellamy Foster, 'Metabolism, Energy, and Entropy in Marx's Critique of Political Economy: Beyond the Podolinsky Myth', *Theory and Society* 35 (2006): 109–56.

26 Marx and Engels, *MECW, Volume 3*, 296.

27 See Thomas Nail, *Marx in Motion: A New Materialist Marxism* (Oxford: Oxford University Press, 2020), ch. 5.

28 Titus Lucretius Carus, *De Rerum Natura (On the Nature of Things)*, ed. Walter Englert (Newburyport, MA: Focus Publishing, 2003), 1.1–30.

29 Ibid., 1.921–30. My transcription of Woolf's annotations/translations from her copy of Lucretius' *De Rerum Natura*, Book I, lines 919–28. Woolf's translations in parentheses.

> *fiet uti risu tremulo concussa cachinnent*
> *et lacrimis* (INSPIRING WIND) *salsis umectent ora genasque.*
> *Nunc age, quod super est, cognosce etclarius audi.*
> *nec me animi fallit quam sint obscura; sed acri*
> *percussit thyrso laudis spes magnameum cor*
> *et simul incussit suavem mi in pectus amorem* (SMITTEN DEEP)
> *Musarum, quo nunc instinctus mente vigenti* (PRICKED HEART)
> *avia Pieridum peragro loca nullius ante* (roam trackless wilds)
> *trita solo. iuvat integros* (VIRGIN) *accedere fontis*
> *atque haurire iuvatque novos decerpere flores.*

30 Ibid., 3.28–30. My transcription of Woolf's annotations/translations from her copy of Lucretius' *De Rerum Natura*, Book III, lines 28–9. Woolf's translations in parentheses.

> *his ibi me rebus quaedam* (THRILLING AWE) *divina voluptas*
> *percipit atque horror* (RAPTURE)*, quod sic naturatua vi,*

31 My transcription of Woolf's annotations/translations from her copy of Lucretius' *De Rerum Natura*. Woolf's translations in parentheses.

> *nam sua cuique, locis ex omnibus, omnia plagis* (SHOCKS) (2.1112)
> *Denique si vocem rerum natura repente.* (SHOCKS) (3.931)
> *vim subitam* (SHOCK) *tolerare: ita magno turbidus* (IN TURMOIL) *imbri* (SEETHING) (1.286)
> *impetibus* (SHOCKS) *crebris, inter dum vertice torto* (CURLING EDDY) (1.293)
> *denique per maria ac montis fluviosque rapacis* (WHIRLING). (1.7)
> *verrunt ac subito vexantia turbine* (WHIRL) *raptant,* (1.279)

32 Ibid., 3.28–30. My transcription of Woolf's annotations/translations from her copy of Lucretius' *De Rerum Natura,* Book III, lines 28–9. See note 30 above.

33 Virginia Woolf, *Mrs. Dalloway* (1925) (Orlando, FL: Harvest/Harcourt, 1981), 68. My italics.

34 Virginia Woolf, *Moments of Being: Unpublished Autobiographical Writings,* ed. Jeanne Schulkind (New York: Harcourt Brace Jovanovich, 1976), 72.

35 Virginia Woolf, *The Essays of Virginia Woolf, Volume 6: 1933–1941,* ed. Stuart N. Clarke (London: Hogarth Press, 2011), 121.

36 Virginia Woolf, *A Passionate Apprentice: The Early Journals (1897–1909),* ed. Mitchell A. Leaska (San Diego, CA: Harcourt Brace Jovanovich, 1990), 393.

37 Virginia Woolf, *Between the Acts* (New York: Harcourt, Brace, 1941), 175.

38 Virginia Woolf, *The Essays of Virginia Woolf, Volume 4: 1925–1928,* ed. Andrew McNeillie (Orlando, FL: Harcourt, 1994), 160.

39 Virginia Woolf, *A Room of One's Own* (1929) (Orlando, FL: Harcourt Brace Jovanovich, 1981), 114. My emphasis.

40 Woolf, *Mrs. Dalloway,* 9.

41 Ibid., 153.

42 Virginia Woolf, *To the Lighthouse* (1927) (Orlando, FL: Harcourt, 1981), 62.

43 Woolf, *Mrs. Dalloway,* 22.

44 Thomas Nail, *Virginia Woolf: Moments of Becoming* (Redwood City, CA: Stanford University Press, under review).

45 See Thomas Nail, *Lucretius I: An Ontology of Motion* (Edinburgh: Edinburgh University Press, 2018); Thomas Nail, *Lucretius II: An Ethics of Motion* (Edinburgh: Edinburgh University Press, 2020); and Thomas Nail, *Lucretius III: A History of Motion* (Edinburgh: Edinburgh University Press, 2022).

46 There is now an extensive literature on this phenomenon. See David Mermin, 'Is the Moon There When Nobody Looks? Reality and the Quantum Theory', *Physics Today* 38, no. 4 (1985): 38–47; Amir Aczel, *Entanglement: The Unlikely Story of How Scientists, Mathematicians, and Philosophers Proved Einstein's Spookiest Theory* (New York: Plume, 2003); and Louisa Gilder, *The Age of Entanglement: When Quantum Physics Was Reborn* (New York: Alfred A. Knopf, 2009).

47 Erwin Schrödinger, 'Die gegenwärtige Situation in der Quantenmechanik', *Die Naturwissenschaften* 23, no. 48 (1935): 844; English translation, 'The Present Status of Quantum Mechanics', in John A. Wheeler and Wojciech H. Zurek (eds), *Quantum Theory and Measurement* (Princeton, NJ: Princeton University Press, 1983), 152.

48 Sean Carroll, *The Big Picture: On the Origins of Life, Meaning, and the Universe Itself* (New York: Dutton, 2016), 100.

49 Max Born (ed.), *The Born–Einstein Letters: The Correspondence Between Albert Einstein and Max and Hedwig Born, 1916–1955* (New York: Walker, 1971), March 1948.

50 See Mermin, 'Is the Moon There When Nobody Looks?'.

51 For a longer introduction and list of these experiments in history, see Aczel, *Entanglement*.

52 Mermin, 'Is the Moon There When Nobody Looks?'. See also Peter Holland, *The Quantum Theory of Motion: An Account of the Broglie–Bohm Causal Interpretation of Quantum Mechanics* (Cambridge: Cambridge University Press, 2004).

53 Holland, *Quantum Theory of Motion*.

54 Arthur Fine, 'Do Correlations Need to be Explained?', in J. Cushing and E. McMullin (eds), *Philosophical Consequences of Quantum Theory: Reflections on Bell's Theorem* (Notre Dame, IN: University of Notre Dame Press, 1989), 175–94; Tanya Bub and Jeffrey Bub, *Totally Random: Why Nobody Understands Quantum Mechanics (A Serious Comic on Entanglement)* (Princeton, NJ: Princeton University Press, 2018); and Bas C. van Fraassen, 'The Charybdis of Realism: Epistemological Implications of Bell's Inequality', *Synthese* 52, no. 1 (1982): 25–38.

55 Henri Bergson, *Matter and Memory*, trans. N. M. Paul and W. S. Palmer (New York: Zone Books, 2005), 104.

56 Karen Barad, *Meeting the Universe Halfway: Quantum Physics and the Entanglement of Matter and Meaning* (Durham, NC: Duke University Press, 2007), 63.

57 Carlo Rovelli, *Reality Is Not What It Seems: The Journey to Quantum Gravity*, trans. Simon Carnell and Erica Segre (New York: Riverhead Books, 2018), 134–5.

III. Process and Pattern

Chapter 5

Ancient Process and Pattern: The Minoan Labyrinth, the Eleusinian Mysteries and Weaving Strings

What is a process? And if matter and motion are processes, why does the world look like relatively solid objects?

We tend to think of processes as things that happen to substances. We imagine, for example, that an object at point A successively transforms as it moves to point B. The standard view is that change occurs when *something* changes into *something* else. Formed substances such as cocoons, one imagines, undergo modifications until they become other formed substances such as butterflies. In this definition, something about the substance remains the same throughout the process of change. The process is secondary or 'accidental' to the substance. This definition assumes something solid and identical, then thinks of change as the *difference* between solid states.

However, this is not the only way to conceive of change. What would it mean to say that there was a change that was not a change *of something*? If matter and motion are ontologically primary in the genealogy of thinkers I have been tracing in this book, how do they account for the stabilisation of indeterminate fluctuations that we see around us?

This chapter and the next aim to trace the history of answers to this question within the tradition of kinetic materialism. The first section gives a philosophical definition of the term 'process' and the second develops the ancient

historical roots of this idea. In the next chapter, I then out-
line the reception of the ideas of process and pattern for
modern kinetic materialists.

What is Process?

A process is an ongoing transformation of matter in motion.
It is a change that changes itself, not a change in something else that remains what it is. Matter is not a continuous or discontinuous substance that changes, and motion is
not a continuous or discontinuous alteration of a substance.
Matter and motion, in the history I am tracing, are *indeterminate processes*.

In a world of processes, there are no fixed substances or
static forms. Matter flows, cycles and circulates in metastable patterns. A metastable pattern is an ongoing process that
restores and repeats itself slightly differently each time, like
a whirlpool or an eddy in water.

Processes are *relational* because they cannot be isolated or
abstracted from a continual transformation without break-
ing the process into discrete pieces. They are *indeterminate*.
In its most radical formulation, a material process has no
beginning or end. If a process had an absolute beginning or
end, its beginning or end would limit the process and intro-
duce something unchanging. In doing so, it would destroy
the process. Absolute beginnings and endings would also be
non-relation for the same reason.

But processes can also create stabilities. The way processes iterate, cycle and weave together sustains metastable
patterns that create the qualities and quantities of the stable
things we see around us. These metastable 'things' result
from ongoing actions that repeatedly iterate. For example,
because heat is constantly dissipating from matter, nothing

can ever be the same thing twice. Due to entropy, all movements of matter in the universe are irreversible. Metastable forms emerge and dissipate because the universe flows from hot to cold. Because of this directionality, the flow of matter can eddy, whirl and entangle itself into stable patterns that give solidity and durability to the world.

By this definition, 'identity' is not a static position or unchanging form but a cycle or habit in indeterminately swerving matter. A thing is what returns to approximately the same place periodically. A difference is not a distinction between two identities but rather a flow or process that cycles into singular recursions. In other words, persistence precedes existence.

For example, when we say that an object changes, such as moving from point A to point B, point A is not a static position but a metastable region formed by iterating indeterminate processes. Matter affects and folds over itself like

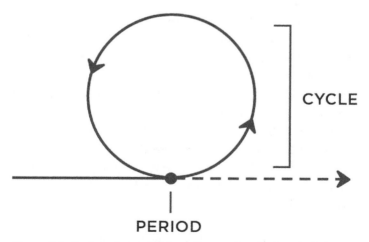

Figure 5.1 Cycle and period. Matter flows and cycles iteratively in a limited area, returning to a similar but never identical spot, before continuing on.

a vortex. Processes cycle, fold and entangle. A particle or point is just a local region where an indeterminate process interacts and intertwines with itself very closely.

As the 'process object' moves from process A to process B, everything changes simultaneously. This *global change* is the relationality I discussed in Chapter 2. When we watch a cocoon turn into a butterfly, everything in the universe is changing together at the same time relative to everything else. Even when things look static, they continue to change relative to everything else.

Movement and stasis, like continuity and discreteness, are not opposed. They are just relative descriptions of processes. The iterative or looping pattern in which matter continually affects and transforms itself is what we can call a 'fold'. Each time a material process affects itself in a fold, it changes. This is why matter is singular, kinetic and iterative. Each fold also weaves together with the motions of others like interlocking vortices.

Over time, folds can be knotted together into durable composites. We do not live in a world of chaotic and incomprehensible flux. We live in a world that follows emergent orders and relatively stable patterns of motion. This is because matter moves together and entrains itself into converging and diverging patterns.

Processes intersect and habitually fold into periodic cycles. These cycles then organise themselves by size and scale into larger loops and layers. To put things simply: Energy flows in, cycles through, and then flows out – *of everything*. Structure and form are the metastable by-products of energetic flows. We should not think of forms as fixed, unchanging entities but as fabrics woven from criss-crossing threads. We might call this fabric of processes a 'field'. A field emerges when a group of processes all fold together, entrained, and give the appearance of a formal unity. Fields are like schools of fish; each alteration weaves into a tessellated and changing whole. A field is a process of processes ordered in such a way as to produce the global effect we call stable reality.

This does not mean there are no relative conflicts between various folds or fields. Larger and more powerful folds can swallow up and entrain smaller ones, as when animals eat one another. Social fields can go to war and unravel one another. Fields also have indeterminacies and instabilities that can make them fall apart or dissolve.

Some fields can even produce relatively stable patterns that conceal their metastable nature and generate an apparent 'conflict' between our perception of them and their processual nature. For instance, rocks tend to move very slowly compared to human lifespans, so they appear stable. However, at larger timescales, rocks flow like rivers across the earth. This was a great insight of general relativity: space and time are relative to fields of motion. Our perception of stability is not wrong; it's just relative. Humans can pretend the world is not relational processes, but they are likely to be continually surprised when all that was supposed to be solid melts into air.

In this chapter and the next, let's take a closer look at some of the ancient and modern ways that the tradition of kinetic materialism has understood the emergence of patterns from indeterminate processes.

The Minoan Labyrinth

As we have seen, Minoan religion strongly emphasised ambiguity and 'uncertainty ... in or between two states of existence'.[1] Such ambiguity *between* states is consistent with

111

the belief that nature is more like a process of metamorphosis than an underlying substance.

As I described in Chapter 2, Minoan religion was also comprised of ecstatic rituals in natural cult settings with no temples or particular gods.[2] The lack of a fixed building or a fixed particular god is also consistent with the idea that the sacred was a process that one could not fix in a single person, space or time.[3]

Furthermore, many scholars have also commented on the processual nature of Minoan art.[4] One of the most cited scholars of Minoan art, H. A. Groenewegen-Frankfort, wrote eloquently on the centrality of movement for the Minoans.

> Cretan art ignored the terrifying distance between the human and the transcendent which may tempt man to seek a refuge in abstraction and to create a form for the significant remote from space and time; it equally ignored the glory and futility of single human acts, time-bound, space-bound. In Crete artists did not give substance to the world of the dead through an abstract of the world of the living, nor did they immortalize proud deeds or state a humble claim for divine attention in the temples of the gods … For life means movement and the beauty of movement was woven into the intricate web of living forms which we call 'scenes of nature'.[5]

Human figures in Minoan art displayed what Groenewegen-Frankfort calls a rhythmic dynamism or 'absolute motion', in which every movement has 'a countermovement within the figure, which makes it appear self-centered but never at rest'.[6] Groenewegen-Frankfort believes that this is evidence for a Minoan worldview based on immanent processes and not transcendent conceptual abstractions.

Another piece of evidence for Minoan process thinking was the religious importance of the *labyrinth*. The origins of the Greek word *labyrinthos* are shrouded in mystery. The most recent linguistic scholarship on the Minoan roots of this word suggests that it may have originally referred to the meandering structure of one or several ritual caves on Crete.[7] The oldest textual evidence for these caves' importance comes from three Linear B tablets recording religious offerings from Knossos, the largest city on Minoan Crete. The tablets say that the Minoans gave one jar of honey to all the gods and one jar and some linen cloth to *da-pu2-ri-to-jo po-ti-ni-ja* or 'the Mistress of the Labyrinth', Potnia. Scholars agree that these tablets gave special reverence to the mistress and her labyrinth by mentioning her separately from the other gods. This would also make the labyrinth one of the most sacred places on Crete.

What do we know about the nature and importance of this labyrinth? Scholars still debate the word's earliest etymology, but we know that from the eighth century BCE onwards, the word described twisted or tortuous pathways.[8] We also know that Minoan and Mycenaean cult architecture is not tortuous, but that the Minoans used sacred caves with twisted passageways. Therefore, several scholars have argued that if the term *da-pu2-ri-to* corresponded to *labyrinthos*, then Potnia's sanctuary should be in a meandering cave.[9] In this way, the meandering structure of Potnia's sanctuary connects to the ecstatic visions of Minoan cave cults and to the legacy of Hellenistic underground labyrinths.[10]

Just as the term 'meander' originated from the name of a winding river in western Anatolia, the 'labyrinth' may have derived from the peculiarities of a Cretan cave noted for its twisted corridors.[11] The classical archaeologist Barbara Montecchi has suggested that the Greeks probably used the term *labyrinthos* to describe anything with tortuous or underground passageways.

Figure 5.2 A sketch by Sieber of the Gortyna Cavern, Crete.

Meander patterns more generally had been used widely on Crete since the Neolithic and had a special significance before the term *da-pu2-ri-to* or *labyrinthos*. The first depiction of the iconic 'labyrinth' (figure 5.3) was adopted by the Mycenaeans around 1250 BCE and mythologised by Homer in the story of Theseus fighting the Minotaur.[12] But the labyrinth image was also an iteration of the older Minoan spiral meander pattern.

How is the labyrinth evidence of a process ontology in Minoan thought? The fact that the most sacred mistress of

Figure 5.3 Silver drachma, Knossos, 300–270 BCE. Obverse: head of Hera, wearing ornamented stephanos, triple-pendant earring and necklace. Reverse: labyrinth, flanked by A–P, ΚΝΩΣΙ(ΩΝ), 'of Knossians', below.

the Minoans oversaw the meandering underground labyrinth suggests that the Minoans thought of the nature of things as similarly tortuous, iterative and open-ended. To worship the divine, one had to journey through the meandering tunnels of Potnia's cave. One had to move from the light down into the darkness to 'see' more clearly without using one's eyes.[13] At the heart of the underground cult site, the Minoans drank a ritual beverage,[14] saw ecstatic visions in the special darkened inner chambers of the Earth, and then returned from the darkness along the same labyrinthine path into the light.[15]

Archaeological evidence of these ecstatic cave rituals is well established, and connects them to the older Neolithic seasonal fertility rituals of death and rebirth.[16] Several Minoan cave scholars have also hypothesised that the experiences of entering, meandering through and exiting the caves functioned as a religious 'transition from one state to another (from dark to light or from one world/condition to another)'.[17] Since the Minoans also used caves as burial sites, it seems likely that their ritual ecstatic journeys into caves were related to death and rebirth.

In one of the most active cult caves on Crete, Psychro, the Minoans inserted beautiful double axes into the stalagmites and created niches in the cave walls where they made offerings.[18] As I discussed in Chapter 1, the double-bladed axe was one of the most important images of the mistress of the labyrinth and expressed well the ambiguity and continually folded process of life and death, light and dark, in its 'visual palindrome'.[19]

Philosophically, all this strongly suggests a process-view of the world where life and death were two dimensions of the same meandering process of nature. We have little or no evidence of major binary oppositions, hierarchical values, or a single god or substance in Minoan culture. One entered and exited the labyrinth-cave via the same place but was transformed in the *process*. The Minoans' ritual emphasis on process may also help make sense of the prevalent spiral meander patterns in Minoan art. The spiral meander pattern has no beginning and no end but is an endless process of iterative transformation similar to life and death.[20] 'The meander is the figure of the labyrinth in linear form', as Carl Kerenyi says.[21]

Although we don't have explicit written evidence that the Minoans had a process-view, the spiral meander is consistent with a worldview that emphasised ambiguity, relationality and processes. In short, the Minoan world was not just indeterminate flux. It also had labyrinthine patterns that folded and ebbed in and out of one another in iterative spirals, just as the cave ritual took one down into the darkness and back up into the light.

In this way, we can hypothesise that instead of *thinking* about the world as either a changing substance or a chaotic flux, the Minoans *performed* the world's folding and unfolding movement in the patterned iteration of the braided labyrinth-cave ritual.

The Eleusinian Mysteries

The Archaic Greeks continued this process-ritual of life and death in their own way in the 'Eleusinian mysteries'.[22] The Eleusinian mysteries were one of the oldest and most widely celebrated rituals in Greek culture.

Eleuthia was a Minoan figure of birth and may have been related to later rituals at Eleusis. So despite the unknown etymology of the pre-Greek word 'Eleuthia', several scholars have conjectured that it was related to Eleusis's rites, because both have underworld labyrinths where one descended into darkness and was reborn into the light.[23] Archaeologists have confirmed the existence of the cave of Eileithya, which Homer recorded near the Cretan city of Amnisos in the *Odyssey*.[24] This was the same cave where the Mycenaeans made cult offerings to Enesidaon/Poseidon, the lord of the underworld.[25]

In this cave Eileithya received 'in Amnisos, a jar of honey',[26] according to the same series of Linear B tablets that recorded 'a jar of honey' for 'the Lady of the Labyrinth'. If the labyrinth was initially a cave, some scholars suggest that Eileithya may have also been the 'Mighty Potnia', who was explicitly invoked by the priests at Eleusis and who 'bore a strong son' from the underworld.[27] The names and precise rituals changed between Minoan Crete and Mycenaean Eleusis, but the Archaic Greeks seem to have preserved at Eleusis the basic idea of a tortuous cave cult dedicated to the process and pattern of ongoing death and rebirth.[28]

Very recent archaeological discoveries even reveal that the Mycenaeans who lived in Eleusis in the twelfth and

Figure 5.4 Drawings of shapes and motifs of pottery from near a platform in front of the Mycenaean Megaron B at Eleusis.

eleventh centuries BCE were still making ritual offerings of burnt pig parts in vessels decorated with the Minoan spiral meander pattern in the exact location of the later temple of Eleusis.[29] In this way, they may have been keeping the memory of an earlier Minoan ritual alive that was passed down to the Archaic Greeks.

The oldest archaeological evidence we have for the Eleusinian mysteries' mythological basis is a ritual cup from the Minoan middle period showing a snake priestess, shaped like the sacrificial tubes that the Minoans used in cave cult activity. The chthonic serpent priestess on the cup is next to two floating female figures, suggesting a trifold movement between the divine, the living and the dead. The priestess is also looking down at a narcissus flower, which strongly connects her to the Greeks' flower maiden they called Persephone. The scholar of Greek religion Carl Kerenyi has argued that Persephone was another name for the Minoan Potnia of the labyrinth who travelled to the underworld and returned to the light.[30] 'The mistress was at the center of the true labyrinth, the underworld; she bore a mysterious son and conferred the hope of a return to the light.'[31]

During the Archaic period, the mystery rites of Eleusis similarly included meandering dances around the 'well of the beautiful dances' (*kallichoron phrear*), from the Greek word *chora*, connected with the unlimited and indeterminate

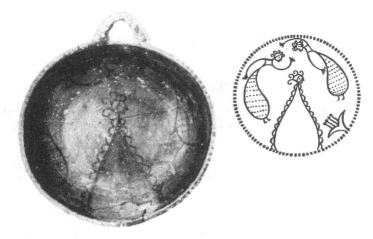

Figure 5.5 Persephone with two companions, on a cup of the Middle Minoan period from the first palace at Phaistos. Archaeological Museum of Heraklion, Crete.

Figure 5.6 Minoan 'snake tubes' found in the sanctuary room at Gournia, Crete. Gournia 1935, left. Gournia 1935, middle; Gournia, 1936, right.

darkness (*khaos*) of the Earth.[32] In Classical Greece, authors
similarly imagined the underworld as a *labyrinthine* path. For
instance, Plato described the underworld as having many
twists and turns, and Proclus said it had a 'three-fold' path.[33]
In this way, the Mycenaeans and Archaic Greeks may have
woven Minoan fertility rituals into the myth of a goddess
who travelled to the underworld and was initially called *Sito
Potnia*, 'Potnia of the Grain', in Linear B inscriptions found
at Mycenae and Pylos.[34] Tablets from around 1400–1200
BCE also refer to 'two queens and the king', which likely
refers to Demeter, Persephone and the god of the dead,[35]
described in the 'Hymn to Demeter' (c. 675–625 BCE).[36]

To sum up this complex historical transition: The
Mycenaeans and Archaic Greeks divided the Minoan
Potnia into the goddess Rhea (the mother goddess of flow)
and her daughter Demeter (of the grain). Then they added
Demeter's daughter, Persephone, 'she who shines in the
dark', who they also called the flower maiden or *Kore*; the
feminine form of *koros*, meaning 'sprout'. Finally, they added
a male god of the underworld. Together, the two queens
and the king tell a similar but distinctly Archaic story of
nature as an endless process of composition, decomposition
and recomposition.[37]

The Archaic 'Hymn to Demeter' sang of a world of
process and endless seasonal patterns. Persephone was out
picking flowers in a beautiful meadow called Nysa, from the
Greek word *nýsta*, meaning 'tiredness, drowsiness, sleepi-
ness'. Notably, Nysa was also the birthplace of Dionysus,
the god of intoxication. In this meadow, Persephone discovered the most 'wonderful, strange, and extraordinary'
narcissus flower, the same flower that the Minoans painted
on their frescoes and the sacrificial cup I mentioned above
(figure 5.5). More specifically, the flower was the sea

daffodil, whose bulb contains a psychotropic and oneiro-genic drug that enhances lucid dreaming.[38] According to the hymn, the flower inspired reverential awe, holiness, honour and worship (*sebas*). It smelled so sweetly that it struck all of the gods in the wide heavens, the whole Earth and the salty seas with astonishment and wonder (*thambe-sas*). They all shook with laughter, joy and playful delight (*athúrō*).[39] In this way, Persephone's drug experience recalls the ecstatic cave rituals on Minoan Crete.

But when Persephone reached for the flower, she was swallowed up by the Earth and taken to the underworld. The flower was a trap laid by Zeus and Gaia. Persephone's

Figure 5.7 Lily fresco. Minoan, 1570–1470 BCE, from Amnisos. Archaeological Museum of Heraklion.

mother, Demeter, who came from Crete,[40] heard Persephone's screams and searched everywhere for her, but none of the gods or birds would say what had happened. Eventually, Hecate and Helios told her, and Demeter went into mourning. She wandered the Earth as an older woman and would not let anything grow.[41] Demeter eventually arrived at the city of Eleusis and took up residence as a nanny with the king. Her hosts offered her wine, but she refused and chose to drink only a 'sacred' (*hósios*) 'herbal potion' (*kukeon*) of 'barley meal, mint, and water'.[42]

The gods finally begged Demeter to come back so that winter would end, and they promised to return Persephone. However, before Persephone left the underworld, Hades, lord of the underworld, sneaked a 'flowing seed', *rhoies kokkon*, into her mouth.[43] According to the Oxford Greek Dictionary and the Greek botanists Theophrastus and Dioscorides, *rhoia* was the 'corn poppy' (*Papaver rhoeas*).[44] This is the same opium-bearing poppy depicted in Minoan art with slits down its sides pouring out opium milk, and adorning the ancient ecstatic goddess of flow, Rhea.[45] It was also the poppy that Demeter held in her hands with her barley bushels in Greek carvings. Indeed, it was also the poppy that the Roman poet Ovid said Persephone was picking in the meadow and that Demeter ate in mourning, and whose milk she fed to the dying child she nursed in Eleusis.[46] According to the hymn, because Persephone ate the poppy, she had to sleep for half of the year in the underworld.

The Greek mysteries of Eleusis were a ritual retelling and performance of this myth. Initiates (*epoptes*), meaning 'those who have seen first-hand', heard the story of Persephone, sacrificed a piglet, walked 18 miles from Athens to Eleusis, fasted, and searched with torches in the dark for Persephone

Figure 5.8 Minoan female figurine with poppy pod crown. Archaeological Museum of Heraklion.

just as Demeter did. Then many entered the darkened *telesterion* or inner 'initiation hall' of the temple. Columns filled the hall like the sacred groves and labyrinthine caves of Crete. There, the initiates drank, just as Demeter did, the 'sacred herbal potion' (*kukeon*) containing a carefully prepared psychedelic barley fungus called ergot, the source of lysergic acid diethylamide (LSD).[47] In this way, the initiates underwent the ego death, transformation and rebirth common in many psychedelic experiences.[48]

Initiates to the mysteries learned the most profound secret of nature – that everything flows (*rhoía*). The goddess of flow (Rhea) mixes (*kukeon*) everything together in cycles of decomposition and recomposition. Everything is reborn as something else. As the Greek poet and mystery initiate Pindar wrote, 'Blessed is he who has seen these things before he goes beneath the hollow earth; for he understands the end of mortal life, and the beginning [of a new life].'[49] The priestesses of Eleusis intended initiates to *undergo* the more general *process* of death and rebirth, like the flowing seeds, sprouts and flowers of Persephone herself.

What does this have to do with the process-view of nature? In these mystery rituals during the Archaic period, there was no religious doctrine or belief about fixed forms or essences, although many later Classical Greeks such as Plato and Pindar predictably offered such transcendent and Orphic interpretations.[50] As an Archaic ritual practice, though, Eleusis emphasised the performative process of destruction and recreation immanent to the natural processes. The ritual was a relational way of knowing through Demeter's psychedelic grain and Persephone's psychotropic poppy.

The great *mystery* was this: Nature comes into being and passes away in a patterned process like the seasonal growth and death of plants. Nature composes, decomposes and recomposes itself endlessly in iterated cycles. Nothing is static. For the Archaic Greeks, the great mystery of nature was not obscure because it transcended nature, but because it was so profoundly immanent to nature and the knower. Processes fold, cycle and weave into the textures and patterns of daily life. The 'mystery' is that we see the *objects* of everyday life but not the *processes*. In the mystery rituals, Demeter's grain revealed (*mustḗrion*) a vision of the immanent processes and patterns of nature by direct gnostic initiation (*mústēs*) with one's eyes closed (*múō*) in the darkened cave.

This is philosophically important because it suggests that, for the Archaic Greeks, being was not an object *of* sight or static knowledge (*epistếmē*), but a sensuous process of becoming and transformation, just like Demeter herself, the iterative 'bringer of the seasons'.[51]

Weaving Strings

Lucretius built on this mythopoetic tradition of process and pattern in his own way. He explicitly connected his materialist philosophy of nature with what 'the ancient, learned poets of the Greeks sang' of as 'mother earth goddess of Cretan Mt. Ida'.[52] However, for Lucretius, only as long as we think of her as the immanent *natural processes of the earth*, and not as a transcendent person who rewards and punishes us, can we 'declare that earth is the mother of the gods'.[53]

The Earth is the creative and destructive source from which and within which all terrestrial bodies flow. Lucretius says that Mother Earth is the 'unlimited and ever-renewing source' of the flows of springs and rivers, the volcanic flows of matter itself, and the wild flows of plants and animals.[54] 'Nature remakes one thing from another, [but] she does not allow anything to be born unless it is aided by another's death.'[55] According to Lucretius, the Earth is the mother of the gods because she contains the 'first threads' (*primordia*), which spread out and weave into many things in many ways and figures.[56] For Lucretius, visible things are pattern-forms that nature weaves from the mixed movements of its various shoots and branches (*semine*), like the sprout-maiden Persephone.[57] Lucretius' image of the weaving mother goddess was not original to him, of course, but probably came directly or indirectly from the Homeric myth of Ariadne, who guided Theseus through the labyrinth of the Minotaur with a string. The names Ariadne and Athena, the Greek goddess of weaving, originated from the original Minoan language and the weaving mistress, Potnia of the labyrinth.[58]

The key theory that Lucretius introduced into this older process-view was that of *simulacra* (images, films or membranes). In his poem, Lucretius describes how nature is woven (*exordia*) together into things (*rerum*) through swerving flows. As matter flows, it weaves different lengths and measures that make things, just like the *textum* of lines and metre in poetry.

Lucretius describes how threads of matter weave together all things and unweave them again. Life and death are two dimensions of the same natural process. In particular, Lucretius uses the word 'simulacra' to describe the way that sensuous things are composed of folded and woven first-threads or *ordia prima*.

I have further shown how the nature of the mind,
and life is braided together from matter,
and is eventually unraveled back into its first-threads,
now I will begin to treat for you what closely relates
to these things: that there exist what we call *simulacra*,
which, like membranes ripped from the outer surface
of things, fly back and forth through the air …

I have shown how nature is woven together
through spontaneous flows of endless motion
and through various formative lengths
which measure the creation of things[59]

For Lucretius, there are no absolutely discrete things – only thread-like processes. Visible things are 'drawn out' and continually woven by matter. The simulacra theory is significant in this material kinetic tradition because it rejects the idea of fixed 'essences'. According to Lucretius, below the manifold and moving simulacra there is no 'real thing' that remains the same despite the peeling away of its membranes.

In this way, simulacra are not copies of things – *things are simulacra*. Things have the forms they do because their simulacra move or *draw out their figures*.

> I say, therefore, that forms and fine figures of things
> are sent out from things, from their outer surface[60]

Strands or strings of matter always figure form.[61] The first-threads are the sprouts of things, and like sprouts, they shed their outer husk, rind, bark or shell (*corpore eorum*)[62] as they move. In this way, moving matter draws out the forms of things like a picture or woven pattern.

> First of all, since in the case of visible things
> many things give off *corpora*, in part scattered loosely,
> as wood gives off smoke, and fire heat,
> and in part more closely woven and compacted, just as at times
> when cicadas shed their smoothly rounded clothing in summer,
> and when calves while being born give off films
> from their outer surface, and likewise when a slippery serpent
> sheds its covering on thorns (for we often see
> bushes decorated with their fluttering body-armor).[63]

Lucretius is quite explicit about the patterned nature of things. Matter (*corpora*) pours out of things (*diffusa solute*) and weaves (*contexta*) figures together like fabrics, clothing (*tunicas*) or armour (*vestem*).[64] When nature weaves these membranes loosely, they scatter like smoke. When nature weaves them more tightly, they come off like a whole shell or snakeskin.

Simulacra are not copies but, like snakeskin or smoke, are entirely material and immanent to things. Lucretius thus jettisons the Platonic theory of model and copy, subject and object, and replaces it with a thoroughly materialist theory of active and diffractive simulacra.[65]

The forms of things are drawn by moving figures, but the flow of the *corpora* cannot be strictly linear because it is habitually (*solerent*) swerving.[66] However, when matter swerves together in certain patterns it can produce the appearance of a relatively linear sequence of images. Therefore, the string figures are not static images flying through empty space. As they move, they diffract with one another and with the air itself. They only preserve their figure when they persevere in their order of motion.

> For why those should fall and separate from things
> more than those which are thin; there is no possibility of
> uttering,
> especially since there exist on the outer surface of things
> *corpora*
> which are many and minute, which can be thrown off in
> the same
> order which they had before and preserve the form of the
> figure,
> and much more quickly, being less able to be impeded
> in as much as they are few and are located right up front.[67]

Matter is continually falling (*cadant*) off things (*recedant*).[68] Still, when it is thrown (*iaci*) off in the same order or pattern (*ordine eodem*), its form is preserved by its kinetic figure (*formai servare figuram*).[69]

In other words, matter is active in the shapes that it traces out in space. Objects have no static form or essence. As their Latin root suggests, objects are what are 'thrown off', *iaci*, '-jected'. But beneath objects there are only processes.

There is only the process of simulacra flying off things in ways that more or less preserve their figure in mid-air.

This is how Lucretius described a world of processes and patterns that weave and unweave everything around us. In the next chapter, we see how Marx, Woolf and a few quantum physicists adopted the ideas of process and pattern from Lucretius and how they applied these ideas to politics, art and science.

Notes

1 Robert B. Koehl, 'The Ambiguity of the Minoan Mind', in Eva Alram-Stern, Fritz Blakolmer, Sigrid Deger-Jalkotzy, Robert Laffineur and Jörg Weilhartner (eds), *Metaphysis: Ritual, Myth and Symbolism in the Aegean Bronze Age. 15th International Aegean Conference, University of Vienna, 22–25 April 2014* (Leuven: Peeters, 2016), 470.

2 See Bogdan Rutkowski, *The Cult Places of the Aegean* (New Haven, CT: Yale University Press, 1986), 149; Oliver Dickinson, *The Aegean Bronze Age* (Cambridge: Cambridge University Press, 1994), 265; and Vesa-Pekka Herva, 'Flower Lovers, After All? Rethinking Religion and Human-Environment Relations in Minoan Crete', *World Archaeology* 38, no. 4 (2006): 590.

3 See Herva, 'Flower Lovers'; Anne Baring and Jules Cashford, *The Myth of the Goddess: Evolution of an Image* (London: Arkana, 2000); R. F. Willetts, *Ancient Crete: A Social History from Early Times until the Roman Occupation* (London: Routledge, 1965); and Marija Gimbutas, *The Gods and Goddesses of Old Europe, 7000 to 3500 BC: Myths, Legends and Cult Images* (Berkeley: University of California Press, 1974).

4 See Carl Kerenyi, *Dionysos: Archetypal Image of Indestructible Life*, trans. Ralph Manheim (Princeton, NJ: Princeton University Press, 1976).

5 Henriette A. Groenewegen-Frankfort, *Arrest and Movement: An Essay on Space and Time in the Representational Art of the Ancient Near East* (London: Faber and Faber, 1951), 186.

6 Ibid., 199.

7 For the suggestion that Linear B *da-pu2-ri-to* came from Linear A (-) *DU-PU2-RE* and that the latter meant 'sacred cave', see Francesco Aspesi, *Archeonimi del labirinto e della ninfa* (Rome: 'L'Erma' di Bretschneider, 2011), 11–37. For different interpretations of Linear A *DU-PU2-RE* and the texts in which it is attested, see recently

Brent Davis, 'Syntax in Linear A: The Word-Order of the "Libation Formula"', *Kadmos* 52, no. 1 (2013): 43 n.6. See also Barbara Montecchi, 'The Labyrinth: Building, Myth, and Symbol', in Eva Alram-Stern, Fritz Blakolmer, Sigrid Deger-Jalkotzy, Robert Laffineur and Jörg Weilhartner (eds), *Metaphysis: Ritual, Myth and Symbolism in the Aegean Bronze Age. 15th International Aegean Conference, University of Vienna, 22–25 April 2014* (Leuven: Peeters, 2016), 165–74. See also Antonis Kotsonas, 'A Cultural History of the Cretan Labyrinth: Monument and Memory from Prehistory to the Present', *American Journal of Archaeology* 122, no. 3 (2018): 367–96.

8 Montecchi, 'The Labyrinth', 166.

9 See Montecchi, 'The Labyrinth', 173; Kotsonas, 'Cultural History'; and Giulia Sarullo, 'The Cretan Labyrinth: Palace or Cave?', *Caerdroia* 37 (2008): 31–40.

10 John C. Montegu, 'Note on the Labyrinths of Didyma', *American Journal of Archaeology* 80, no. 3 (1976), 304–5.

11 Ovid compares the Labyrinth's passageways built by Daidalos with the winding course of the Meander river. Ovid, *Metamorphoses Volume 1: Books 1–8*, trans. Frank Justus Miller, ed. G. P. Gould (Cambridge, MA: Harvard University Press, 1984), VIII.162–8.

12 Montecchi, 'The Labyrinth', 170.

13 Loeta Tyree, 'Diachronic Changes in Minoan Cave Cult', in Robert Laffineur and Robin Hägg (eds), *POTNIA: Deities and Religion in the Aegean Bronze Age* (Liège and Austin, TX: Université de Liège and the University of Texas at Austin, 2001), 39–50 (43).

14 For fascinating evidence of drinking vessels in ecstatic cave ritual, see ibid.

15 There are many possible causes of ecstatic states in Minoan caves, including drugs, music, dancing and even reduced oxygen levels in certain cave spaces. See Yafit Kedar, Gil Kedar and Ran Barkari, 'Hypoxia in Paleolithic Decorated Caves: The Use of Artificial Light in Deep Caves Reduces Oxygen Concentration and Induces Altered States of Consciousness', *Time & Mind: The Journal of Archaeology, Consciousness and Culture* 14, no. 2 (2021): 181– 216, https://doi.org/10.1080/1751696X.2021.1903177.

16 Tyree, 'Diachronic Changes'; Martin P. Nilsson, *The Minoan-Mycenaean Religion and Its Survival in Greek Religion*, 2nd edn (Lund: Gleerup, 1950), 470.

17 Tyree, 'Diachronic Changes', 44.

18 Ibid., 41.

19 Cited in Koehl, 'The Ambiguity of the Minoan Mind', 471.

20 Ibid., 469–70.

21 Kerenyi, *Dionysos*, 90.

22 Baring and Cashford, *Myth of the Goddess*, 377–85.

23 Nilsson, *The Minoan-Mycenaean Religion*, 521; R. F. Willetts, *Cretan Cults and Festivals* (Abingdon: Routledge, 2013). See also Fritz Schachermeyer, *Die Minoische Kultur des alten Kreta* (Stuttgart: Kohlhammer, 1967), 141–2.

24 Homer, *Odyssey Volume 1: Books 1–12*, trans. A. T. Murray, ed. George E. Dimock (Cambridge, MA: Harvard University Press, 1919), XIX.189.

25 Tablet KN Ma 719. Cited in Bernard C. Dietrich, *The Origins of Greek Religion* (Bristol: Bristol Phoenix Press, 1974), 221.

26 Tablet KN Gg 705. Cited in Sarullo, 'Cretan Labyrinth', 38.

27 Dietrich, *Origins*, 167. See note 198 on the evidence for this phrase being used during the rites of Eleusis.

28 Dietrich says that 'a strong memory of a divine son and a cave cult have survived in Eleusis'. Ibid.

29 Michael B. Cosmopoulos, 'Cult, Continuity, and Social Memory: Mycenaean Eleusis and the Transition to the Early Iron Age', *American Journal of Archaeology* 118, no. 3 (2014): 401–27; and Michael B. Cosmopoulos and Deborah Ruscillo, 'Mycenaean Burnt Animal Sacrifice at Eleusis', *Oxford Journal of Archaeology* 33, no. 3 (2014): 257–73. Kerenyi makes a strong but more speculative case for mystery cults in Mycenean Megaron B. See Carl Kerenyi, *Eleusis: Archetypal Image of Mother and Daughter*, trans. Ralph Manheim (Princeton, NJ: Princeton University Press, 1967), 18–25.

30 Kerenyi, *Dionysos*, 106–7. See also John Chadwick, *The Mycenaean World* (Cambridge: Cambridge University Press, 1976), 84–101; and Ann Suter, *The Narcissus and the Pomegranate: An Archaeology of the Homeric Hymn to Demeter* (Ann Arbor, MI: University of Michigan Press, 2002), 162. I also agree with some degree of continuity between the Minoan Potnia and Persephone.

31 Kerenyi, *Dionysos*, 118.

32 Ibid., 93. See also Kerenyi's discussion of the dance around the well at Eleusis, called the *kallichoron phrear* or 'well of the beautiful dances'. Kerenyi, *Eleusis*, 70–2.

33 Plato, *Phaedo*, ed. and trans. Chris Emlyn-Jones and William Preddy (Cambridge, MA: Harvard University Press, 1917), 108 A; Proklos, *In Platonis Rem publicam commentar: Vol. II*, ed. Wilhelm Kroll (Teuber, 1901), 85 6: *triodous*.

34 George E. Mylonas, *Mycenae and the Mycenaean Age* (Princeton, NJ: Princeton University Press, 1967), 159.

35 In Crete, Poseidon was often given the title wa-na-ka (*wanax*) in Linear B inscriptions. He was the king of the underworld, and his title E-ne-si-da-o-ne indicates this. See Dietrich, *Origins*, 181–5.

36 'Wa-na-ssoi, wa-na-ka-te (to the two queens and the king). Wanax is best suited to Poseidon, the special divinity of Pylos. The identity of the two divinities addressed as wanassoi, is uncertain.' Mylonas, *Mycenae and the Mycenaean Age*, 159. The two queens and the king may refer to Demeter, Persephone and Poseidon. See Chadwick, *The Mycenaean World*.

37 The Archaic version is more patriarchal. See Suter, *The Narcissus and the Pomegranate*.

38 'The narkissos flower figures prominently in Minoan art, on a sacrificial knife and wall paintings and a golden ring, probably the emblem of a shamanic priestess, depicting women as "bee ladies" experiencing a vision, and even a ceramic plate showing a Persephone snake-goddess with her flower. We can identify it as *Pancratium maritimum*, the sea daffodil, of the amaryllis family.' Carl A. P. Ruck, 'Mixing the *Kykeon*, Part 3', *ELEUSIS: Journal of Psychoactive Plants and Compounds* New Series 4, (2000), 23. See also Carl A. P. Ruck, *Sacred Mushrooms of the Goddess: Secrets of Eleusis* (Berkeley, CA: Ronin, 2006), 78–9; Maha M. Soltan, Ahmed R. Hamed, Mona H. Hetta and Ahmed A. Hussein, 'Egyptian *Pancratium maritimum* L. Flowers as a Source of Anti-Alzheimer's Agents', *Bulletin of Faculty of Pharmacy, Cairo University* 53, no. 1 (2015): 19–22; and Stephen LaBerge, Kristen LaMarca and Benjamin Baird, 'Pre-sleep Treatment with Galantamine Stimulates Lucid Dreaming: A Double-blind, Placebo-controlled, Crossover Study', *PLoS One* 13, no. 8 (2018): e0201246.

39 Homer, 'Hymn to Demeter', in *The Homeric Hymns*, ed. and trans. Susan Shelmerdine (Newburyport, MA: Focus Publishing, 1995), lines 5–15.

40 First century BCE Diodorus of Sicily also says that the mysteries came from Crete, V.77.3. Cited in Kerenyi, *Eleusis*, 24.

41 In *The Narcissus and the Pomegranate*, Ann Suter argues that the myth of Demeter was added to the older myths of Persephone in which Persephone accomplished the journey on her own without Demeter or Hades.

42 Homer, 'Hymn to Demeter', lines 205–10.

43 Ibid., lines 270–375.

44 See Theophrastus, *Enquiry into Plants*, trans. Arthur F. Hort (London: Heinemann, 1916), Book 9, chapter 12, line 4; Pedanius Dioscorides, *De Materia Medica*, Book 4, chapter 64. According to Carl Ruck and Danny Staples, the chambered pomegranate is also a surrogate for the poppy's narcotic capsule, with its comparable shape and chambered interior. Carl A. P. Ruck and Danny Staples, *The World of Classical Myth: Gods and Goddesses, Heroines and Heroes* (Durham, NC: Carolina Academic Press, 2001).

45 For a translation of *rhoia kokkon* as 'corn poppy', see Henry G. Liddell and Robert Scott, *Greek–English Lexicon, With a Revised Supplement* (Oxford: Clarendon Press, 1996). This is in contrast with the Greek word for pomegranate, which is *rodi*. The ancient Greek botanist Theophrastus explicitly gave the name *rhoias* to the corn poppy that grows among the barley. 'Another kind of poppy is that called rhoias, which is like wild chicory, wherefore it is even eaten: it grows in cultivated fields and especially among barley. It has a red flower, and a head as large as a man's finger-nail. It is gathered before the barley-harvest, when it is still somewhat green. It purges downwards.' Theophrastus, *Enquiry into Plants*, 9.12.4.

46 See Ovid, *Fasti*, trans. James G. Frazer, ed. G. P. Gould (Cambridge, MA: Harvard University Press, 1931), Book IV, April 12: The Games of Ceres.

47 See R. Gordon Wasson, Albert Hofmann and Carl A. P. Ruck, *The Road to Eleusis: Unveiling the Secrets of the Mysteries* (Berkeley, CA: North Atlantic Books, 2008). The most recent edition of this book contains an appendix by a chemist who demonstrates that one only needs wood ash to make the ergot potion psychoactive without toxicity. For a discussion of the hard archaeological evidence for the use of psychedelic ergot in the mysteries, see Brian Muraresku, *The Immortality Key: The Secret History of the Religion with No Name* (New York: St Martin's Press, 2020). The archaeological evidence was discovered at an Eleusian-based mystery cult in Spain. See Jordi Juan-Tresserras, 'La arqueología de las drogas en la Península Ibérica: una síntesis de las recientes investigaciones arqueobotánicas', *Complutum* 11 (2000): 261–74; and E. Pons et al., *Mas Castellar de Pontós (Alt Empordà). Un complex arqueològic d'època ibèrica (Excavacions 1990–1998)* (Girona: Museu d'Arqueologia de Catalunya, 2002), 481.

48 For a description of what such an experience might have been like, see Michael Pollan, *How to Change Your Mind: What the New Science of Psychedelics Teaches Us About Consciousness, Dying, Addiction, Depression, and Transcendence* (New York: Penguin, 2018).

49 Pindar, fragment 137, in *Nemean Odes, Isthmian Odes, Fragments*, ed. and trans. William H. Race (Cambridge, MA: Harvard University Press, 1997), 384–5.

50 Plato described his mystery experience as 'in a state of perfection'. Plato, *Phaedo*, 250b–c.

51 Homer, 'Hymn to Demeter', line 192.

52 Titus Lucretius Carus, *De Rerum Natura (On the Nature of Things)*, ed. Walter Englert (Newburyport, MA: Focus Publishing, 2003), 2.600–12.

53 Ibid., 2.655–60.

54 Ibid., 2.590–9.

55 Ibid., 1.263–4.

56 Ibid., 2.653–4.

57 Ibid., 2.686–7.

58 See Kerenyi, *Dionysos*, 99–122. Linguist Robert S. P. Beekes has also supported Ariadne having a pre-Greek origin; specifically being a Minoan from Crete.

59 Lucretius, *De Rerum Natura*, 4.28.

60 Ibid., 4.42–3.

61 Donna J. Haraway, *Staying with the Trouble: Making Kin in the Chthulucene* (Durham, NC: Duke University Press, 2016).

62 Lucretius, *De Rerum Natura*, 4.43.

63 Ibid., 4.54–62.

64 Ibid., 4.55, 4.57, 4.58, 4.61.

65 See also Gilles Deleuze, *Logic of Sense*, trans. Mark Lester and Charles Stivale (New York: Columbia University Press, 1990), 266–79. On the question of how to interpret Lucretius' optical theory, see Thomas Nail, *Lucretius II: An Ethics of Motion* (Edinburgh: Edinburgh University Press, 2020), 153.

66 Lucretius, *De Rerum Natura*, 2.221.

67 Ibid., 4.65–71.

68 Ibid., 4.65.

69 Ibid., 4.68, 4.69.

Chapter 6

Modern Process and Pattern: Marx's Motion, Woolf's Waves and Quantum Gravity

Marx's Forms of Motion

The primary focus of Marx's masterwork, *Capital: Critique of Political Economy, Vol. 1: The Process of Capitalist Production* (1867), was to understand the nature of social motion and the *process* of production. Marx's fundamental methodological orientation to modern society was process-oriented.[1] Society, like all sensuous nature for Marx, was nothing other than matter in motion. Social motions are neither predetermined substances nor random events but emergent and dialectical patterns. Various patterns of movement emerge, persist, dissipate and re-emerge historically.

Modern society moves according to what Marx calls a *Bewegungsform*, 'form of motion' or 'motion-form'.[2] The process of material production creates social patterns or forms of circulation. Matter in motion, as Marx says following Lucretius, produces moving forms, including the 'value-form' that defines capitalism.

Indeed, Marx described the philosophical aim of *Capital* like this: 'it is the ultimate aim of this work to reveal the economic law of motion [*Bewegungsgesetz*] of modern society'.[3] But what is a law of motion? Law, for Marx, is something laid down through a process or pattern of motion. Law cannot pre-exist someone actively laying it down through movement. If Marx believed that law was natural and fixed, this would be an ahistorical and non-dialectical 'ultimate aim' of nature. This would not fit with his theory of the indeterminate swerve that we read in his dissertation.

The whole of part one of *Capital* is a careful theory of how the movement of the material production process becomes 'settled' into patterns of constant exchange and custom, resulting in value or 'abstract labor time'. Once settled, however, these patterns can become unquestioned habits. It may 'seem' *as if* these patterns had always been there or that they were natural forms of motion. We may even *act as if* these patterns are universal laws. But this is not the case.

As Marx says in the postface of *Capital*: only after the social 'forms of motion' have become settled historically can we determine the real effective motions.[4] Only after the *historical movement* is complete can the *conceptual form* present the 'real form of motion' in contrast to the 'mystical' Hegelian 'idea' which acts as if it were prior to history.[5] Because matter is an indeterminate process, Marx cannot believe in Newtonian natural law or Hegelian dialectical law.[6]

Instead, Marx got his theory of law from Lucretius. Marx made this clear in his doctoral thesis when he wrote that '*declinatio atomi a recta via* is the law'.[7] The *swerve* of the atom is the *lex atomi*, or the law of the atom. For Marx, law is simply the tendency for matter to move indeterminately and dialectically through non-predetermined motions. In other words, the law of matter is to swerve away from all fixed laws. This is a strange law, indeed.

However, just because the movement of matter is unpredictable does not mean it is random. For Marx, law is explicitly immanent to the sensuous appearance and qualities of the matters *in process*. 'For the study of nature', Marx says, 'cannot be pursued in accordance with empty axioms and laws.'[8] An empty law is a formal law that transcends its historical patterns. Law, for Marx, must be a kinetic form or settled pattern specific to the qualities and domain of its sensuous appearance. Marx's theory here is related to Hegel's description of law as the 'source of a self-kindling movement',[9] but Marx goes beyond this with the materialist law of the atom's self-swerving. 'That is, it is no external condition of motion but being-for-self, immanent, absolute movement itself.'[10]

Only in Lucretius' materialism of the swerve does the law and form of motion become purely immanent. There is no interaction *between* law and motion. Law is *nothing other than* the immanent form or pattern of motion. As Marx writes about capitalism, 'The life process of capital consists only in its movement as value constantly expanding, constantly multiplying itself.'[11]

Just as the moon traces real patterns in the sky that we cannot see all at once without time-lapse photography, so there are also social forms or laws of motion that we cannot see all at once without the aid of historical concepts. Marx says, 'Just as the heavenly bodies always repeat a certain movement, once they have been flung into it, so also does social production, once it has been flung into this movement of alternate expansion and contraction.'[12] The patterns or laws of social motion are real and immanent, but because they are processes and not discrete things, we tend to mistake the product for the process. This mistake is the central problem that Marx calls 'fetishism'. It occurs when we think that there is a natural hierarchy of one thing over another.

For Marx, economic value fluctuates and changes not because it is 'accidental and purely relative',[13] but because there is a secret form of motion (*Form einer Bewegung*) operating beneath the cover of the apparent discreteness of the commodity-form:

> These magnitudes vary continually [*wechseln beständig*], independently of the will, foreknowledge and actions of the exchangers. Their own movement [*Bewegung*] within society has for them the form of a movement [*Form einer Bewegung*] made by things, and these things, far from being under their control, in fact control them.[14]

Social value, for Marx, is ultimately defined by the process of metabolism or continual interchange (*wechseln beständig*) that I discussed in Chapter 2. Economic values move *as if* they had no qualities, but they still have a specific form of motion. For example, the circulation of capitalist value still depletes the soil, kidnaps people from their homes, and treats women's bodies as wombs to reproduce labour. Social patterns of motion follow hierarchical ways of thinking and acting as if they, too, were eternal principles.

A social form of motion is the hanging-together of collective action in interdependent patterns. What at first appeared to political economists as an 'accidental and purely relative' form of motion, Marx exposed as a specific structure with its own pattern of motion defined by the production and movement of economic value:

> All the different kinds of private labour which are carried on independently of one another; and yet, as spontaneously developed branches of the social division of labour, are in a situation of all-round dependence on one another [*allseitig von einander abhängigen*].[15]

Together, all these seemingly random individual motions are part of a larger pattern of motion that hangs together on all sides.

The secret of what Marx calls 'commodity fetishism' is that there are laws, forms or patterns of motion that both structure the birth of value and hide beneath the apparent randomness and arbitrary structures of domination and economic exploitation. If we want to create a world without domination, for Marx, we need to see that everything is flexible processes and patterns and not fixed hierarchies. There are no eternal laws, only emergent dialectical ones. This does not necessarily tell us what to do, but lets us know that we have the freedom to experiment with patterns that might be better. The social conflict or antagonism is between those who believe in fixed forms and those who want to experiment with more flexible patterns.

Woolf's Waves and Webs

Woolf also drew directly from Lucretius in her understanding of the world as processes and patterns. Woolf wanted to describe the nature of things as they are below the surface of solid objects, which she says float like corks in the fluid medium of 'reality'. In Woolf's moments of being, she described the world and herself as waves, curled up, iterated and diffracted.

'I see myself as a fish in a stream; deflected; held in place', she wrote.[16] Woolf felt in these moments not like a generic flux but as a particular metastable formation. She was like a fish, a process or flow whose movement with and against a moving current gave the appearance of stability. Woolf said she 'fancies [herself] afloat, [in an element] which is all the time responding to things we have no words for – exposed to some invisible ray'.[17] The world and her body continually changed with one another in a fluid medium of imperceptible relational patterns.

Writing, for Woolf, runs up against the limits of representation precisely because of the fluid nature of reality. How can a static word or idea possibly capture a fluid process? The challenge of writing, for Woolf, was how to say the unsayable. How can we *become* part of the process *through* writing without representing the process *with* writing?

The problem of reconciling *process* and *solidity* haunted Woolf her whole life.

> And now is life very solid or very shifting? I am haunted by the two contradictions. This has gone on forever; goes down to the bottom of the world – this *moment* I stand on. Also, it is transitory, flying, diaphanous. I shall pass like a cloud on the waves. Perhaps it may be that though we change; one flying after another, so quick, so quick, yet we are somehow successive, and continuous.[18]

For Woolf, the world is neither discrete solid objects, what she called the 'cotton wool' of everyday life, nor some vitalistic force. Instead, she wrote that her 'constant idea' or 'philosophy' was that the world is moving *patterns* whose metastable formations are wholly immanent with the diaphanous flows that fly so quickly through them.[19] This is why Woolf was fascinated by waves and even named one of her novels *The Waves*. A wave is curled and folded up into a relatively solid moving object, but is also a continuously changing fluid process at the same time. Woolf was not just a stream of consciousness writer. For her, *everything* was streaming.

Woolf discovered these moving patterns beneath the surface of appearances in her moments. She wrote that 'Behind the cotton wool is hidden a pattern; that we; I mean all human beings; are connected with this; that the whole world is a work of art; that we are parts of that work of art.'[20] Woolf says she uncovered the world as a patterned work of art below the apparent discreteness of things. This pattern is not a question of *beauty*, as Woolf put it, but of *being*.[21] Aesthetic patterns are real patterns, not merely subjective states. Patterns are what weave together all the qualities that make up sensuous reality. This is why Woolf says '"The proper stuff of fiction" does not exist; everything is the proper stuff of fiction', because everything is woven of the same process-reality.[22]

In her moments, Woolf described 'a revelation of some order', 'some real thing behind appearances'.[23] But we should note that the patterns are immanent to the appearances, for Woolf, and not beyond them. Appearances are not false, but just the tips of the icebergs of reality. The appearances of discrete things are like 'little corks that mark a sunken net'[24] of something 'immeasurable; a net whose fibres pass imperceptibly beneath the world'.[25] The 'real thing' is not a discrete object but rather an expansive and entangled pattern weaving the world together. These patterns or nets, as Woolf called them, are the 'invisible ... backgrounds', or 'scaffolding', 'behind' but *immanent to* the world.[26] They are the processes that sustain metastable appearances – the flows upon which the corks of people and objects float. These background patterns 'prove that one's life is not confined to one's body and what one says and does; one is living all the time in relation to certain background rods or conceptions. Mine is that there is a pattern hid behind the cotton wool.'[27] The patterns beneath the cotton wool are not discrete substances or visible things, but this does not mean that they are metaphysical, for Woolf. The patterns are invisible, but not because they are beyond reality. They *are reality* itself, as a web or net of relational processes. As processes, though, they often elude us. Art is needed to reveal them.

Woolf described the kinetic nature of these patterns similarly in her essay 'Modern Fiction'.

> Look within and life, it seems, is very far from being 'like this'. Examine for a moment an ordinary mind on an ordinary day. The mind receives a myriad impressions — trivial, fantastic, evanescent, or engraved with the sharpness of steel. From all sides they come, an incessant shower of innumerable atoms; and as they fall, as they shape themselves into the life of Monday or Tuesday, the accent falls differently from of old; the moment of importance came not here but there.[28]

Life does not occur as a series of accurate empirical descriptions. Instead, it contains innumerable material processes whose iterative movements produce and sustain the forms of life and reality itself. Depending on the relations and the swerve of matter, daily empirical life comes together even though the falling matter itself *is not something empirical*.

This description is a fascinating interpretation of Lucretius — whom Woolf, her Latin tutor, her husband, her father, her brother and many in her Bloomsbury cohort all read closely and discussed.[29] Woolf's description of reality above is nearly identical to that of Lucretius in *De Rerum Natura*. Woolf says that matter falls into the 'shape' of things, just as Lucretius described the movement of simulacra weaving into the figures and forms of things. In this way, Woolf and Lucretius both agree that the discrete stuff we see with our eyes is only the surface shape of a deeper kinetic pattern produced by continually folded and woven flows of simulacra.[30]

Woolf, drawing on Lucretius, thus gave the novelist the same task that Lucretius gave to the poet-philosopher: to describe these unknown kinetic patterns.

Let us record the atoms as they fall upon the mind in the order in which they fall, let us trace the pattern, however disconnected and incoherent in appearance, which each sight or incident scores upon the consciousness. Let us not take it for granted that life exists more fully in what is commonly thought big than in what is commonly thought small.[31]

For Woolf, modern fiction aims to trace these material-kinetic patterns and processes behind life's cotton wool. This is a fantastic proposal. Woolf essentially tells us that art's challenge is not to describe or represent the empirical world but to describe its material processes and patterns. As she says in her autobiography, the description of these patterns is performatively part of them: 'I make it real by putting it into words.' Life exists in these small, invisible, background processes, just as much as in the macroscopic world of people and things.

Quantum Gravity

Lucretius was also an important precursor to process understandings of objects in physics. The quantum theorist Carlo Rovelli argues that 'The very idea of Einstein's, that the existence of atoms is revealed by the Brownian motion of minute particles immersed in a fluid, may be traced back to Lucretius.'[32] Einstein proved that solids, liquids and gases are not static objects but metastable processes. He called this the 'kinetic theory of matter', and Lucretius described it two thousand years earlier in his theory of simulacra.

Rovelli also recognises that one of the consequences of Lucretius' theory of indeterminacy is that objects are processes and vibrational patterns.

Due to this indeterminacy, in the world described by quantum mechanics, things are constantly subject to random change. All the variables 'fluctuate' continually, as if, at the smallest scale, every thing was constantly vibrating. We do not see these omnipresent fluctuations only because of their small scale; they cannot be observed at large scale, as when we observe macroscopic bodies. If we look at a stone, it stays still. But if we could see its atoms, we would observe them to be always now here and now there, in ceaseless vibration. Quantum mechanics reveals to us that the more we look at the detail of the world, the less constant it is. The world is not made up of tiny pebbles. It is a world of vibrations, a continuous fluctuation, a microscopic swarming of fleeting microevents.[33]

The idea that nature is indeterminate relational processes woven together into emergent patterns and cycles is a core aspect of Rovelli's 'relational' interpretation of the quantum theory of gravity. In quantum physics, what appear to be relatively static classical objects, molecules and atoms, are metastable states of vibrating energy fields. Rovelli argues that the same is true for space and time.

'The world is in a ceaseless process of change', down to the most fundamental processes of matter and motion in quantum physics.[34] It is also possible that indeterminate and relational quantum processes are even more fundamental than space and time itself. This is the theory called quantum gravity. As Rovelli writes,

We can think of the world as made up of *things*. Of *substances*. Of *entities*. Of something that *is*. Or we can think of it as made up of *events*. Of *happenings*. Of *processes*. Of something that *occurs*. Something that does not last, and that undergoes continual transformation, that is not permanent in time. The destruction of the notion of time in fundamental physics is the crumbling of the first of these two perspectives, not of the second. It is the realization of the ubiquity of impermanence, not of stasis in a motionless time.[35]

If quantum processes are genuinely fundamental, as Lucretius argued long ago, then even space and time are emergent properties of matter in motion. Our entire universe unfolded itself into stars, galaxies and black holes from an indeterminately high-energy region at the moment of the Big Bang.

Rovelli even argues that the Big Bang did not come from nothing (just as Lucretius argued) but from a previous universe that contracted into a tiny region of quantum space and then exploded into our universe. He and other physicists call this the 'big bounce' theory, and many physicists hypothesise that the birth and death of the cosmos has occurred innumerable times before. If quantum gravity is correct, our universe may begin to contract again at some point, and so on in a grand cycle of creation and destruction similar to that described by the ancient Minoan labyrinth ritual – but on a much larger scale than they imagined.

If there were no determinate space, time, matter, physical laws or fundamental fields before the Big Bang, then everything came to be through *processes* and *patterns* of relational iteration. For Rovelli, this is the source of Lucretius' philosophy and ethics: 'There is [in Lucretius] a deep love of nature, a serene immersion within it; a recognition that we are profoundly part of it; that men, women, animals, plants, and clouds are organic threads of a marvelous whole, without hierarchies.'[36] Rovelli correctly understands that Lucretius' physics of interwoven processes is also related to his ethical theory, which rejects all fixed ontological hierarchies.

Similarly, Rovelli proposes to visualise the immanent feedback patterns between quantum fields as loops or bubbles in space. In the late nineteenth century, Michael Faraday was the first to think of the magnetic field as continuous 'lines of induction'.[37] In quantum-field theory, excitations in these energetic field lines produce a 'vortical whirling'[38] or 'bubbling'[39] effect on the surface of the field, causing it to interact with itself and with other fields. In other words, the field lines 'loop' back over themselves in cycles of continual feedback and transformation.

This idea is the basis of the 'loop' in what Rovelli calls 'loop quantum gravity'. Loop quantum gravity treats these energy loops as composing the primary fabric of spacetime itself. 'The closed lines that appear in the solutions of the Wheeler–DeWitt equation are Faraday lines of the gravitational field', Rovelli argues.[40] The assemblage of all these active quantum-field loops produces a 'spin foam network', so-called because its loops weave together the texture of space itself. Physicists call it a '"[f]oam" because it has surfaces that meet on lines, which in turn meet on vertices, resembling a foam of soap bubbles'.[41]

In short, the idea is that the feedback patterns of quantum processes are primary ontological aspects at the heart of space and time itself. Objects are first and foremost processes that fold into loops and foams. As Rovelli explains,

> In the world described by quantum mechanics, there is no reality except in the relations between physical systems. It isn't things that enter into relations, but rather relations that ground the notion of thing. The world of quantum mechanics is not a world of objects: it is a world of events. Things are built by the happening of elementary events. As the philosopher Nelson Goodman wrote in the 1950s, with a beautiful phrase: 'An object is a monotonous process.' A stone is a vibration of quanta that maintains its structure for a while, just as a marine wave maintains its identity for a while, before melting again into the sea.[42]

Figure 6.1 Energy loops and folds together to generate space, similar to the way soap forms bubbles.

Matter and motion weave the bubbling fabric or sea within which spacetime and objects are iterated patterns. The looping nature of objects means that, as the philosopher and physicist Karen Barad writes, matter 'intra-acts with itself (and with other particles)'.[43] Quantum theory is not just a theory of indeterminate processes but of intra-active and diffractive patterns where processes affect themselves and others to produce a tangle of metastable particles. If this is the case, there are not relations between *relata* in space and time, but rather processes weave spacetime. This is why Barad calls it 'spacetimemattering'.[44]

This is also what 'entropic gravity theory' proposes. In the quantum vacuum, which we discussed in the first chapter, the higher the degree of entanglement, the higher the entropy of a specific region. Thus the measure of entropy in a given region, according to physicist Sean Carroll, 'turns out to be naturally proportional to the area of the region's boundary. The reason isn't hard to understand: field vibrations in one part of space are entangled with regions all over, but most of the entanglement is concentrated on nearby regions.'[45]

The higher the entanglement, the higher the entropy, and the closer the fluctuations are to one another. The weaker the entanglement, the more distant. Thus the laws of spacetime in general relativity, according to this theory, emerge from entropic and entangled processes.[46] In short, the conclusion of loop quantum gravity and entropic gravity theories is that spacetime is an emergent pattern of quantum processes. This is a big idea and requires more experimental evidence before general relativity and quantum theory can be reconciled in a quantum theory of gravity. But if quantum theory can be experimentally reconciled with general relativity, it will also fit well into the trajectory of kinetic materialism traced in this book.

Now, we have covered a lot of history in this book relatively quickly. So in the next chapter, I will conclude with a brief summary of the key takeaways from this history.

Notes

1 For a full argument, see Thomas Nail, *Marx in Motion: A New Materialist Marxism* (Oxford: Oxford University Press, 2020).

2 See Karl Marx and Frederick Engels, *Marx-Engels-Gesamtausgabe, Vol. 10* (Berlin: Dietz, 1975), 17, 98, 103, 108.

3 Karl Marx, *Capital: A Critique of Political Economy, Vol. 1*, trans. Ben Fowkes (New York: Penguin, 1990), 92.

4 Ibid., 103.

5 Ibid.

6 John P. Burkett, 'Marx's Concept of an Economic Law of Motion', *History of Political Economy* 32, no. 2 (2000): 381–94.

7 Karl Marx and Frederick Engels, *Marx & Engels Collected Works, Volume 1: Karl Marx 1835–43* (London: Lawrence and Wishart, 1975), 472–3. Hereafter *MECW*.

8 Ibid., 68.

9 G. W. F. Hegel, *Science of Logic* (1812) (New York: Humanities Press, 1966), 2:365.

10 Marx and Engels, *MECW, Volume 1*, 474.

11 Karl Marx and Frederick Engels, *Marx & Engels Collected Works, Volume 35* (London: Lawrence and Wishart, 1975), 315.

12 Marx, *Capital, Vol. 1*, 786.

13 Ibid., 126.

14 Ibid., 167–8.

15 Ibid., 168.

16 Virginia Woolf, *Moments of Being: Unpublished Autobiographical Writings*, ed. Jeanne Schulkind (New York: Harcourt Brace Jovanovich, 1976), 80.

17 Ibid., 115.

18 Virginia Woolf, *A Writer's Diary: Being Extracts from the Diary of Virginia Woolf*, ed. Leonard Woolf (1954) (Orlando, FL: Harcourt, 1982), 138. My italics.

19 Woolf, *Moments of Being*, 72.

20 Ibid.

21 Woolf, *A Writer's Diary*, 85.

22 Virginia Woolf, *The Essays of Virginia Woolf: Volume 4: 1925–1928*, ed. Andrew McNeillie (Orlando, FL: Harcourt, 1994), 164.

23 Woolf, *Moments of Being*, 72

24 Woolf, *Moments of Being*, 116.

25 Virginia Woolf, *The Waves* (1931) (Orlando, FL: Harvest/Harcourt, 1959), 214.

26 Woolf, *Moments of Being*, 73.

27 Ibid.

28 Woolf, *Essays, Vol. 4*, 160.

29 See Susanna Rich, '"De undarum natura": Lucretius and Woolf in *The Waves*', *Journal of Modern Literature* 23, no. 2 (1999–2000): 249–57; and James Morland, 'The Influence of Lucretius on Unity in *The Waves*', *Virginia Woolf Bulletin* 38 (2011): 23–6.

30 For a full commentary and analysis of this, see Thomas Nail, *Lucretius I: An Ontology of Motion* (Edinburgh: Edinburgh University Press, 2018); and Thomas Nail, *Lucretius II: An Ethics of Motion* (Edinburgh: Edinburgh University Press, 2020).

31 Woolf, *Essays, Vol. 4*, 161.

32 Carlo Rovelli, *Reality Is Not What It Seems: The Journey to Quantum Gravity*, trans. Simon Carnell and Erica Segre (New York: Riverhead Books, 2017), 37.

33 Ibid., 132.

34 Carlo Rovelli, *The Order of Time*, trans. Erica Segre and Simon Carnell (New York: Riverhead Books, 2018), 97.

35 Ibid.

36 Rovelli, *Reality*, 39.

37 P. M. Harman, *Energy, Force, and Matter: The Conceptual Development of Nineteenth-Century Physics* (Cambridge: Cambridge University Press, 1982), 80; and L. Pearce Williams, *The Origins of Field Theory* (New York: Random House, 1966), 88, 124.

38 Frank Close, *The Infinity Puzzle: Quantum Field Theory and the Hunt for an Orderly Universe* (New York: Basic Books, 2011), 43.

39 Rovelli, *Reality*, 187.

40 Ibid., 161.

41 Ibid., 187.

42 Ibid., 135.

43 Karen Barad, *Meeting the Universe Halfway: Quantum Physics and the Entanglement of Matter and Meaning* (Durham, NC: Duke University Press, 2007), 14.

44 Ibid., 179.

45 See Sean Carroll, *Something Deeply Hidden: Quantum Worlds and the Emergence of Spacetime* (Boston: Dutton, 2019).

46 For more on a review of entropic gravity and its relationship to loop quantum gravity, see Lee Smolin, 'Newtonian Gravity in Loop Quantum Gravity', *Perimeter Institute for Theoretical Physics*, 29 October 2018, https://arxiv.org/pdf/1001.3668.pdf (accessed 28 April 2023).

Conclusion

In this book, I have presented the reader with a unique genealogy of what I call kinetic materialism. Instead of defining matter and motion as determinate objects moving on a pre-given background of space and time, I have showcased a history of thinkers who, in my reading, understood matter and motion as *indeterminate relational processes*.

As I said in the introduction, my motivation for writing this history was to show the operation of a long and diverse philosophical tradition that has rejected the hierarchy of beings and the passivity of matter and motion. I did this in part because I still worry that if critical philosophy retains an explicitly or implicitly human-centric view of the world, superior to or separate from matter, conceptual and practical hierarchies will remain entrenched in theoretical and daily practice. In my opinion, indeterminacy, relationality and process are three of the most important ideas from history that can help keep us away from metaphysical delusion and naturalised hierarchies.

The takeaway from this history is not that we should necessarily repeat *exactly* what any of these thinkers did or thought. Different histories and geographies call for novel responses. This is why I organised the book around the three ideas of 'indeterminacy', 'relationality' and 'process'. Each thinker in this history articulated and expressed these ideas in their own way. Our experimentation with them today may be as different from these thinkers as they were different from one another.

I would also like to stress again that kinetic materialism does not tell us what we *should* do.[1] The purpose of my writing this history is to inspire the reader by showing them what kinds of ideas and practical consequences *can* follow for religion, art, politics and science if matter and motion are indeterminate relational processes.

Caution is important, though. What might practically result from these ideas today *could* be worse than what we want to avoid. This is possible, but I think it's much more probable that these ideas will help people see what is poison and what is remedy for themselves, without the unnecessary blindfold of metaphysics and hierarchy. There are no guarantees in politics, but if we want to reduce domination and ecological destruction, we have to be free and willing to experiment more responsively in a world of indeterminate processes. Indeed, it might help us to learn from what others in this alternative tradition, and outside the West, have done and thought.

Unfortunately, the tradition of kinetic materialism has travelled underground in Euro-Western geography, like a mushroom mycelium.[2] It has often lain dormant, or fruited only briefly in odd places before going back underground. Occasionally, radical naturalists, communists and feminists such as Lucretius, Marx and Woolf have picked and eaten its fruits. More frequently, though, it has only been glimpsed from a distance, misidentified or stepped on by various metaphysical philosophies that have preserved ontological hierarchies explicitly or implicitly.

The genealogy of kinetic materialism is a 'dark' antiquity/ modernity buried by so-called periods of historical 'enlightenment'. The Ionian enlightenment of the sixth century

BCE, the Renaissance of the fifteenth and sixteenth centuries, and the modern enlightenment of the seventeenth–nineteenth centuries all waged war against the darkness of kinetic materialism. I call the early formation of kinetic materialism 'dark antiquity' because the Western tradition associated indeterminacy with dirt, earth, chaos, void, caves, forests, evil, night and death. Matter and motion are what all these terms have in common and why the European tradition placed them at the bottom of its hierarchy.

Kinetic materialism is also dark because of its emphasis on non-representational, performative and relational ways of knowing. In the West's prevailing idealism, performative knowledge often does not count as 'real' because it is not purely objective and illuminated by rational thought.

Kinetic materialism pops up across religion, art, science and politics because it rejects the ontological division between culture, nature and 'different' knowledge domains. Matter, in this tradition, is a shape-changer and a parodic trickster. As the French philosopher George Bataille playfully wrote, 'It is clear that the world is purely parodic, that each thing seen is the parody of another, or is the same thing in a deceptive form.'[3]

The genealogy I present in this book is not a story of progressive development from primitive to superior articulations of kinetic materialism. Instead, I have tried to highlight how each thinker or tradition expressed a different historical and thematic way of adopting a similar indeterminate relational materialism. Kinetic materialism traverses religion, mythology, poetry, philosophy, politics, literature and science. It has taken me many years of study, writing and teaching to parse all the candidates and transmission lines, some of which are still uncertain. But this is the first book in which I have tried to connect all the dots.

I have also tried to create an iteration of this kinetic materialism in my own philosophy of movement. But there are so many more ways it can be done and has been done in history and around the world. I hope my future research will take me deep down these other paths as well. I also hope that Western philosophers can recognise some of the assumptions they have made about matter and motion and the dangers of the path they have chosen. It is important to remember that there are alternative pathways within their own tradition. But there are similar dangers and alternative pathways in other cultures and geographies as well. May the fruits of all these alternatives be picked and eaten, inspiring us to experiment everywhere with caution and care.

Notes

1 On the question of ethics, see Thomas Nail, *Lucretius II: An Ethics of Motion* (Edinburgh: Edinburgh University Press, 2020).
2 For an excellent book on mushrooms, ecology and capitalism, see Anna Tsing, *Mushroom at the End of the World: On the Possibility of Life in Capitalist Ruins* (Princeton, NJ: Princeton University Press, 2021).
3 Georges Bataille, *Visions of Excess: Selected Writings, 1927–1939*, ed. and trans. Allan Stoekl (Minneapolis: University of Minnesota Press, 1985), 5.

Index